I

'UFO Religion is a delightful story about an idea, one that preys upon the emotions and excites the imagination of each and every one of us. From its humble origins in the airship mysteries of nineteenth-century liars' clubs and newspaper hoaxes, Gregory Reece chronicles the notion of alien spacecraft and visitors from outer space as this has evolved and been elevated into an article of faith for the bizarre host of conspiracy theorists, utopian dreamers, alleged abductees and contactees we find in our midst today. Reece's vision is a refreshing and humorous reminder that no matter how whimsical their origins and rationales might seem, our strangest ideas can take on lives of their own through their primal grip on our hopes, fears, and dreams. In Reece's world, UFOs and alien visitors are every bit the children of our minds as they are children of the stars. They emerge as a most serious – yet entertaining – subject of *human* concern.'

David Beisecker, Associate Professor of Philosophy,
University of Nevada, Las Vegas

'Greg Reece's UFO Religion engagingly captures that sense of mystery and wonder that drives ufologists to undertake their research. The book is a thorough and impressive analysis of UFO investigations and of supposed alien encounters. In an entertaining and readable style, Reece guides the reader through a maze of possibility and makes many intriguing links between science and religion *en route*. UFO Religion is an important book for anyone who is interested in the idea that our planet has hosted extraterrestrial visitors: or in what Carl Gustav Jung called "flying saucer cults".'

Susan J. Palmer, Professor of Religious Studies, Dawson College,
Montreal, and author of Aliens Adored: Rael's UFO Religion

'*UFO Religion* is both an informed study of the subject and a thoroughly enjoyable read. While several excellent studies of belief in extraterrestrial visitation are now available, for those unfamiliar with this fascinating area *UFO Religion* is certainly the book to start with. Gregory L. Reece covers a broad range of material with a light and deftly humorous touch. I have no doubt that his book will become a firm favourite with students. I am also confident that even those who, up to this point, have not been particularly interested in UFO belief will enjoy this carefully researched, well-written and accessible book.'

Christopher Partridge, Professor of Contemporary Religion and Co-Director of the Centre for Religion and Popular Culture, University of Chester, and editor of UFO Religions

'In his exploration of the complicated and diverse world of UFO culture, Gregory L. Reece communicates a sense of wonder at the extent of the human imagination and our ability to tell powerful and lasting stories about the mysteries of the world around and beyond us. Reece takes his readers on a fascinating excursion from Alabama to Roswell, New Mexico and back again, with many entertaining detours along the way. Stories of alien abductions and distant worlds, he argues, are responses to the infinite possibilities of life and reflect the best and worst of our fears and hopes for the future. He reminds us that we are, after all, "children of the space age", and so it seems fitting that we cannot decide whether to transform the world or to escape it, to feel hope about the future or terror. It is impossible to reach the end of this book without acquiring a much deeper understanding about the enduring human obsession with UFOs.'

Sarah M. Pike, Professor of Religious Studies, California State University, Chico, and author of New Age and Neopagan Religions in America

UFO Religion

INSIDE FLYING SAUCER CULTS AND CULTURE

Gregory L. Reece

I.B. TAURIS
LONDON · NEW YORK

Published in 2007 by I.B.Tauris & Co Ltd
6 Salem Road, London W2 4BU
175 Fifth Avenue, New York NY 10010
www.ibtauris.com

In the United States of America and Canada
distributed by Palgrave Macmillan, a division of St Martin's Press
175 Fifth Avenue, New York NY 10010

ISBN 978 1 84511 451 0

A full CIP record for this book is available from the British Library
A full CIP record is available from the Library of Congress

Library of Congress Catalog Card Number: available

Typeset in Palatino by JCS Publishing Services, www.jcs-publishing.co.uk
Printed and bound in the United States

Contents

Illustrations

All the photographs are by the author

This book is for Olivia

Acknowledgments

Thanks to Alex Wright of I.B.Tauris for understanding that a book about UFOs would be the logical sequel to a book about Elvis.

Thanks to Sam for inspiring my dormant imagination time after time.

Thanks to Kristen for listening to me talk about flying saucers for over twenty years and for reading the manuscript and thinking that it was funny.

Aurora is the effort
Of the Celestial Face
Unconsciousness of Perfectness
To simulate, to Us.

– Emily Dickinson

Introduction

The aurora borealis is not something that is usually seen in Alabama, that land of whippoorwills and dogwood trees. The northern lights have no business way down south. Yet I possess a distinct childhood memory of sitting on the front porch of my oldest brother's mobile home watching the northwest sky shimmer with hues of red and gold. Aurora borealis, sandstorms in the American west lifted high into the atmosphere and reflecting the setting sun, atomic fire, Jesus on the clouds of glory, alien invasion, the end of the world; the possible explanations running together like the yellow sky running into the red; a sickening feeling in my stomach and the knowledge that whatever it was, even if it was Jesus himself, it was not going to be good; knowing with terrifying certainty that the mobile home, tied to four posts that my father had cut in the woods just for the purpose, couldn't even stand up to the tornado it was meant to protect against much less an apocalyptic wind blowing Jesus fire and Martian death rays.

In my childhood both Jesus and UFOs were absolutely terrifying. I didn't want to see them, didn't really even want to hear about them. But, of course, hear about them I did: Jesus, on Sunday morning when my Great-Aunt Francis would attempt to save me from the godlessness of my own household by taking me with her to church so that I could learn the terrifying truth about hellfire and damnation, Jesus' return from the grave and his coming on the clouds of glory to take me in his arms and carry me home, and UFOs every other day of the week

Among the first graders in my class in 1973, stories of UFOs were exchanged like baseball cards. The most famous story of all that year, talked about by children and adults alike, was the story of Jeff Greenhaw, police chief of nearby Falkville, Alabama. Investigating a reported UFO landing, Greenhaw claimed that he had encountered a five-and-a-half-foot tall creature dressed from head to toe in a shiny metallic uniform. When Greenhaw stopped his car the thing approached, moving forward with the slow jerkiness of a robot. Suddenly, it turned and ran away from the car with strange spring-like bounds. The creature moved so quickly that Greenhaw was not able to keep pace with it in his patrol car. While most adults snickered at the picture Greenhaw had taken as showing nothing more than a prankster wrapped in tin foil, it was to my six-year-old self an absolutely terrifying image that continues to give me a shiver when I look at it today. (Even though as an adult I am obliged to say that it looks, in all honesty, like a prankster wrapped in tin foil.) One might imagine that if this thing came after you there would be no running away. Bounding after you at speeds faster than a police patrol car, this creature would give you no chance of escape.

Indeed, for me, it hasn't.

I cannot shake off my fascination with grainy images of flying saucers and foil-wrapped spacemen. Lights in the night sky continue to intrigue me, though I have never again seen anything as dramatic as my memory makes the night of my childhood apocalypse. I am entranced by the stories of abductees and by those who have witnessed UFOs, by those who claim communication with beings from another realm of reality and by those who scour the desert for evidence of crashed saucers or alien remains, and in this fascination I am far from alone.

From Mexico City to Moscow come reports of flying saucers and flying cigars, abductions and cattle mutilations. As prevalent as appearances of Jesus or the Virgin Mary, the sightings appear to fill the witnesses with a sense of awe similar to that produced by those other inexplicable images, a sense of awe, a sense of wonder, a sense of holy terror in the face of the unknown. Crowds gather to gaze skyward at flickering lights hovering above city streets just as they gather around an underpass image of the Virgin growing like mold on a concrete wall. Religions spring up around sightings as they sprang up around Jesus, that ancient visitor from the stars with his own band of contactees. For me, even now as in childhood, it all runs together – that smiling Jesus and the tin-foil alien – the hound of heaven leading the Men in Black in a midnight chase across the alien landscapes of my life.

I don't want to imply that UFOs are all shock and awe, however, as if I have let my fear of foil-wrapped aliens get the best of me, as if I can't see that Greenhaw's ET looks more like a baked potato than a representative of some extraterrestrial civilization, as if I can't tell a pie plate tossed in the air in front of a camera from an invading armada of tentacled space creatures. If we take this too far we begin to shape hats from tin foil in order to protect ourselves from the mind-control rays emanating from the alien mother ship, and that is not a place that most of us really want to go. Indeed, one of the great things about flying saucers is that in photos they do often resemble pie plates. Remains of saucer wreckages sometimes do look like kite parts. Contactees who claim to have boarded flying saucers or channeled extraterrestrial brain waves sometimes do come off looking like kooks. In other words the awe and wonder associated with flying saucer sightings comes wrapped in tin foil, clothed in the absurdly laughable, accompanied by kooks (in the best sense of that word) and cons (the best sense of that word too). Fear and laughter, awe and irony, dire warnings, tin foil, and pie plates: this strange juxtaposition is what makes ufology such a compelling subject.

♦ ♦ ♦

This book is an exploration of a broad spectrum of ufological phenomena, including both the frightening and the funny. The central focus of the book is on the religious aspects of UFO culture, but in order to keep the religious aspects of ufology in context it also covers a lot of material that might not usually be classified as religious. Saucer culture is a deeply interrelated web of claims and beliefs, with strands of that web reaching far beyond UFO culture into the nooks and crannies of popular culture and popular religion. I have not been able to follow all of those strands, but I have followed a lot of them.

The first part of this book is a look at what is sometimes called 'Nuts and Bolts Ufology.' Nuts and Bolts ufology, so the claim goes, is not interested in religious or metaphysical claims about flying saucers. Instead ufologists of this ilk are interested in the scientific study of the phenomenon, and look at the 'nuts and bolts' of the affair. I'll be so bold as to say that there is plenty of religious awe and irony found in the nuts and bolts of ufology, whether its proponents are aware of it or not. Even without being so bold, however, it is fair to say that it is hard to understand the more explicit forms of religious ufology without first understanding the nuts and bolts variety. Part One is divided into four chapters. Chapter 1 examines visual sightings of flying saucers, UFOs, and whatnot. Chapter 2 examines saucer crash stories, Chapter 3 takes a look at the more conspiratorial theories concerning saucers, and Chapter 4 explores the abductee phenomenon.

The second part of the book is devoted to those individuals and groups who are usually designated as 'contactees.' These are the people that the 'nuts and bolts' folks usually refer to as the 'lunatic fringe.' One chapter is devoted to the classic contactees of the 1950s. The other chapter looks at the religious groups and institutions that arose from the contactee movement.

Part Three of the book examines the 'Ancient Astronaut' branch of ufology, those who look to ancient texts and monuments as evidence that extraterrestrials visited our planet in the distant past. One chapter examines the modern history of this idea. The other looks at religious movements that incorporate some or part of the ancient astronaut concept.

◆ ◆ ◆

The challenges that arise in attempting to understand UFO cults and cultures are also the things that make the quest exciting. To believe in UFOs, and especially to see some religious significance in them, is to be outside the religious mainstream and, with just a few exceptions, to be outside the religious mainstream is to be free of enforced doctrine and orthodoxy. In that climate dissent and novelty flourish. Diversity complicates the research for books such as this, and is what makes it fun. Likewise to be outside the mainstream is, by definition, to be marginal and marginalized. It is to be without the resources of religious institutions; it is to be outside the academy; it is to be beyond the interest of most publishers. Obscurity also complicates the research for books such as this one. It also contributes to the fun.

The people and ideas that this book chronicles are reminiscent of what Charles Fort (more on him later) called the damned. For Fort, the damned were all of those reports, and testimonies, and facts that were ignored by science because they did not fit into the system. They were a diverse set of claims about fish falling from the sky, strange lights in the heavens, spontaneous combustion, and teleportation. They were also the obscure items, hidden away on an interior page of newspapers down below the fold, or found in the kind of rags that respectable individuals would not read. It was their diversity and their obscurity that drew Fort to them. He wished to bring them to light, if for no other reason than to show that the world is stranger than we ever imagined. He wished to bring them to light, for without such all would be monolithic and mainstream. I feel the same way about the people and ideas upon which this book is focused. The world of human ideas and beliefs, hopes and dreams, fears and dreads, is more interesting, more frightening, more cracked than most of us imagine.

I'll let Fort himself close this introduction and introduce the weirdness to follow.

A PROCESSION of the damned.
By the damned, I mean the excluded.
We shall have a procession of data that Science has excluded.
Battalions of the accursed, captained by pallid data that I have exhumed, will march. You'll read them – or they'll march. Some of them livid and some of them fiery and some of them rotten.
Some of them are corpses, skeletons, mummies, twitching, tottering, animated by companions that have been damned alive. There are giants that will walk by, though sound asleep. There are things that are theorems and things that are rags: they'll go by like Euclid arm in arm with the spirit of anarchy. Here and there will flit little harlots. Many are clowns. But many are of the highest respectability. Some are assassins. There are pale stenches and gaunt superstitions and mere shadows and lively malices: whims and amiabilities. The naïve and the pedantic and the bizarre and the grotesque and the sincere and the insincere, the profound and the puerile.

UFO religion

A stab and a laugh and the patiently folded hands of hopeless propriety.

The ultra-respectable, but the condemned, anyway.

The aggregate appearance is of dignity and dissoluteness: the aggregate voice is a defiant prayer: but the spirit of the whole is processional.

The power that has said to all these things that they are damned, is Dogmatic Science.

But they'll march.

The little harlots will caper, and freaks will distract attention, and the clowns will break the rhythm of the whole with their buffooneries – but the solidity of the procession as a whole: the impressiveness of things that pass and pass and pass, and keep on and keep on and keep on coming.

The irresistibleness of things that neither threaten nor jeer nor defy, but arrange themselves in mass-formations that pass and pass and keep on passing. (Fort, 1974: 3–4)

Let's not forget the little tin-foil alien, Mr. Fort. He deserves a place in your parade too.

PART ONE

Nuts and Bolts

1

Sightings

In the middle of a week-long conference of UFO devotees from all over the world, discussing everything from sightings to saucer crashes to abductions, the invitation to a night-time sky watch in the Mojave Desert was both tantalizing and a little frightening. It was tantalizing not necessarily because it offered me the chance to see an actual UFO but because it offered me the chance to find out a little more about the people in attendance at the conference, the true believers. It was frightening for the very same reason. The hand-lettered invitation to the sky watch indicated that it was not an official UFO Congress event. There was no indication of who was organizing the sky watch or of what their motivation might have been. In other words, attending the sky watch meant that I would travel out into the Mojave Desert in the middle of the night to rendezvous with a group of strangers of which the only thing I knew for certain was that they were very devoted UFO believers. I didn't know if the event would include meditation, signal flares, or peyote. I didn't know if the participants were the nice, safe kind of UFO devotees or the nice, but a little scary kind of UFO devotees, both of which I had discovered in rather large numbers at the International UFO Congress. I had met ambassadors from peaceful galactic federations as well as those whom I suspected were on the other side of the galactic cold war. Either way, it was an opportunity I would not have dreamed of missing.

Instead of car pooling with other participants I opted to drive myself to the designated meeting spot. I suppose I thought that if the others did not appear friendly my own car would give me a better chance of escape (though looking back on it, it is doubtful that my rental car could have escaped one of those tin-foil-suited aliens known to outrun police cruisers). I arrived before anyone else. With no moon to light up the sands this part of the Mojave Desert was without a doubt the darkest place that I have ever had the fortune to visit. As a consequence the night sky was stunning to behold. The stars were thicker than I have ever seen them, as if the heavens had been dusted with confectioner's sugar. In the distance I could see an approaching series of bright lights illuminating the scrub brush on the hills around me. I watched them closely with anticipation and more than a little apprehension. The lights offered few clues as to the nature of those who were approaching. Suddenly the lights went out, disappearing behind a ridge. The desert in its absolute quiet and incredible darkness seemed for the moment like an alien landscape, the stars close enough to touch; then, all around me, bright lights, shattering the darkness.

— Airships —

One of the earliest written accounts of a sighting of an extraterrestrial craft appeared in the November 19, 1896 edition of the *Stockton Evening Mail*. The details of this report, along with other nineteenth-century newspaper reports of aerial craft, are wonderfully elaborated by Daniel Cohen in *The Great Airship Mystery: A UFO of the 1890s* (1981) and by Wallace O. Chariton in *The Great Texas Airship Mystery* (1991). On this occasion the *Stockton Evening Mail* reported that, while driving his buggy through the countryside near Stockton, California, Colonel H. G. Shaw claimed to have encountered what could only be described as a grounded spacecraft. One hundred and fifty feet in length and twenty-five feet in diameter, the vessel came to a sharp point on both ends. The only distinguishing feature on its smooth metallic surface was a large rudder. The vessel itself might not have been enough to indicate the extraterrestrial nature of the craft had it not been accompanied by three strange beings. Nearly seven feet tall and extremely thin, they approached Shaw while emitting what he described as a strange warbling noise. They examined Shaw's horse and buggy and tried, unsuccessfully, to force Shaw to accompany them aboard their craft. Lacking the physical strength to force him along they rushed back aboard without their prey. Within moments the ship rose from the earth and sped away into the sky. Shaw expressed his opinion that the beings were from Mars. He further surmised that they may have been sent to California to abduct an earth dweller for some unknown purpose, perhaps diabolical. Could it be that their inability to overpower Shaw would be enough to discourage any more such attempts? (If so, the world is lucky that I was not their first victim. Knowing that running was futile, I would have played 'possum and no doubt been taken easily back to Mars, a ready candidate for whatever experiments they wished to perform.)

Some five months later, on April 10, 1897 the *St. Louis Post-Dispatch* reported yet another encounter with a strange craft and its even stranger inhabitants. W. H. Hopkins reported that he had encountered a grounded craft on the outskirts of Springfield, Missouri. The vessel, much smaller than the one seen earlier by Shaw, was twenty feet long and only eight feet in diameter. It was metallic in appearance and apparently driven by three large propellers. The crew of this craft was also quite different from that reported by Shaw. While Shaw described the crew of the craft as being distinctly non-human, Hopkins described a meeting with near-perfect specimens of the human race. In place of Shaw's tall, gangly creatures he found a stunningly beautiful nude woman accompanied by a likewise nude bearded man. Hopkins attempted to establish contact with these beings through signs and gestures, hoping to discover their point of origin. After much effort he finally made them understand his question. In response they pointed upward and uttered something that sounded like the word 'Mars.' After this brief revelation they climbed back aboard the vessel, which quickly rose and disappeared into the distance (Cohen, 1981: 59–60).

These reported encounters with Martian visitors were originally published as part of a wave of sighting stories that appeared in American newspapers in the last years of the nineteenth century. These reports, usually of unidentified lights in the sky but also of visible craft in flight and of craft and crew on the ground, began in November 1896 and continued off and on through the turn of the century. The first sighting report was made on November 18, 1896 when the *Sacramento Bee* and the *San Francisco Call* reported that a bright, slow-moving light had been observed over Sacramento, California on the evening of November 1. Witnesses estimated the altitude of the light at a thousand feet. Some were reported as saying that they could see a dark shape behind the light. One witness, identified as R. L. Lowery, had his attention drawn upward when he heard a voice from above call out a command to increase elevation in order to avoid crashing into a church steeple. Lowery reported, in what was no doubt meant as a wink to the reader, that there was no church in the area so he supposed that they must have been referring to the tower of a nearby brewery. Glancing up, the witness reported a bright light mounted on the front of an airship that seemed to be powered by two men pedaling furiously, as if on bicycles. Above the bicycles Lowery made out a box that seemed to hold passengers and, above that, a cigar-shaped object. Others reported hearing the sound of singing coming from the sky. Most witnesses, however, were recorded as reporting only a bright, slow-moving light (Chariton, 1991: 17–18).

Whether stories included rather elaborate descriptions of flying bicycles or simply consisted of reports of strange lights, newspapers thereafter began referring to the reports, which quickly spread across California, the Midwest, and Texas, as airship sightings. Coming in the years before the success of the Wright brothers at Kitty Hawk and before zeppelins were truly viable as a means of travel, the idea that an airship carrying passengers had passed overhead would obviously have been a thrilling thought. In that age of rapid technological progress it also must have seemed entirely possible. Indeed, despite the report of Shaw's encounter with Martians, which was published on the day after the original sighting, most theories concerning the airship attributed its nature and origins to a terrestrial source. Most suspected, not visitors from another planet, but the technological success of some inventive genius who, for whatever reason, was not yet ready to make his breakthrough public. This theory was so prevalent that it was reported in April of 1897 that Thomas Edison was forced to issue a strongly worded statement denying his responsibility for the airship sightings that had been reported all over the nation in the previous year and a half (Chariton, 1991: 93).

Though California airship stories seem to have been a thing of the past by early 1897, this was not the case in other parts of the country. On February 2, 1897 the *Omaha Bee* reported that the airship had appeared over Hastings, Nebraska on the previous day. From there newspapers throughout Nebraska and the Midwest began running airship stories, the details of which became more and more fascinating. On April 16, 1897 the *Table Rock Argus* reported that a group of anonymous but reliable witnesses had observed the airship sailing above them. Much to their surprise they could see many passengers on board the craft, among them two women, one of whom seemed to be bound to a chair while the other waited on her; a man kept watch over the prisoner with a revolver. Before the witnesses could think to contact the authorities, however, the craft had sped off into the distance (Cohen, 1981: 51).

The *Albion Weekly News* reported that two witnesses had been surprised to see the airship crash just inches from where they were standing. As quickly as it had crashed, however, the craft had disappeared, leaving only a lone man in its place. When asked about the airship the man removed a small object from his pocket and informed them that he had the ability to shrink the airship down to pocket size – which, of course, explained why no one had been able to locate it when grounded (Cohen, 1981: 51). The *Wilsonville Review* reported that their editor had seen the airship and heard a voice call out 'Weiver Eht Rof Ebircsbus.' Read from right to left the message becomes clear (Cohen, 1981: 52).

There were also plenty of reports of hoaxes that made their way into the newspapers. The *Dallas Morning News* of April 17, 1897, for example, reported that on the previous evening three boys had attached a kerosene-soaked cotton ball to the leg of a turkey buzzard. The ball was ignited, the bird was released, and the 'airship' was aloft. It was reported that the boys were thrilled when they heard shouts of 'Look it's the airship' coming from their fellow citizens. They weren't so thrilled (or maybe they were) when the buzzard landed on the roof of the high school, setting it ablaze (Chariton, 1991: 143–4).

UFO religion

What was the cause of these stories? Was there really something inexplicable flying over North America at the end of the nineteenth century? There is no record of a successful airship from that era and surely it would have been impossible, not to mention irrational, to keep such a thing secret. Certainly many of the reports were simply jokes. Newspapers of the day were not nearly as averse to printing completely fabricated tales as truth as they purport to be today. Most of the readers would have been in on the joke. Likewise, it is possible that many of the reported sightings were based on real eye-witness testimony of phenomena purely explicable by such ordinary fare as optical illusions, misidentified natural objects, and pranks. I suppose that the fact that offers the greatest challenge to the idea that something significant, either a new invention or an extraterrestrial craft, was actually seen in 1896 and 1897 is the way in which the story simply disappeared from the newspapers. The issue was never resolved. The newspapers simply moved on to other things and the story was forgotten. The reports didn't make it into the history books. Surely, if the stories had been backed by reality, or if the newspapers themselves had believed the stories to be real, they would have pursued the issue more thoroughly. Instead, once the joke was over and everyone had had their turn to laugh, the airship wave of 1896–7 simply dropped out of memory. The unidentified flying object of the nineteenth century simply went away. It was not to go away forever, however, for some fifty years later there were new reports of sightings, reports of other unidentified flying objects, which began to be appear around the world. Students of the new phenomena would uncover the old stories of airships and begin to see in them the precursor of the events of their own day. Now, however, airships were to be replaced by flying saucers and the extraterrestrial hypothesis was to reign supreme.

— Saucers —

In June of 1947 newspapers reported the story of Kenneth Arnold of Boise, Idaho. Arnold related in a press conference that he had observed strange flying objects while piloting his small plane over Washington State. At an altitude of 9,000 feet he observed nine

1. Saucer parking in Rachel, Nevada near Area 51

crescent-shaped objects moving at great speed. The objects were flat and highly reflective. Arnold described their movement as reminiscent of a saucer skipping across the surface of water. The term 'flying saucer' thus entered the English lexicon, though not at that point with clear extraterrestrial connotations. As a matter of fact, Arnold would later say that he had originally assumed that his sighting had been of terrestrial guided missiles.

Whether such missiles were of US or foreign origin was an open question. In June of 1947 the memory of World War II, Hiroshima, and Nagasaki was clear in everyone's mind. In addition, the developing cold war had curtailed any sense of safety that might have arisen with the defeat of Japan and Germany. The Soviet Union was evolving into a potentially bigger threat. The concept of 'flying saucer,' as it was first used in the summer of 1947, was not clearly associated with alien visitors in the way that it would be in

UFO religion

Hollywood movies within just a few short years. In 1947 most people who read a report of Arnold's press conference would have thought, not of Martians, but of the very human threats they perceived all around them.

The same was true of the now famous Roswell, New Mexico UFO crash that was reported shortly after the Arnold sighting. According to the July 8, 1947 *Roswell Daily Record*, the Roswell Army Air Base announced in a press release that the base had recovered a flying saucer. In contrast to later re-evaluations of what happened at Roswell, the original report made no assumptions about the extraterrestrial nature of the saucer. The recovery of a flying disc would have raised more worries about Soviet invasion than about visits from space people.

Though the Roswell story was soon forgotten following the military's insistence that they had recovered nothing more than a weather balloon, sighting reports continued to multiply, covered by both small and large newspapers around the US and around the world. With the growing number of sightings reported by the media, theories of their nature and origin also abounded. Many of these would be articulated, not in the mainstream media, but in limited-edition books and pulp periodicals, by individuals with what were sometimes extremely provocative theories, some extraterrestrial and some not. Many of the non-extraterrestrial theories would serve to make the idea of alien visitors seem somewhat reasonable.

For example, Meade Layne published *The Ether Ship and its Solution* in 1950 and proposed that flying saucers were actually phenomena originating in Etheria, an alternative dimension that exists alongside our own while remaining unknown to our senses. Saucers materialize and de-materialize in what appears to be empty space. The craft become visible as their atomic motion is slowed. Sightings of Ether Ships, according to Layne, have been recorded throughout history and constitute the historical origins of much ancient mythology and religion. Etherians are not gods, however. They are mortal beings just like us, though more advanced in their technological and spiritual knowledge and capabilities. Their purpose in visiting our reality is to expand their own understanding of the universe and to share some of their truth with citizens of our own realm. Layne believed it possible for individuals with very developed psychic powers to contact and interact with the Etherians; some Etherians have been trapped in our dimension when their Ether Ships malfunction. On some occasions, Layne reports, crashed craft, along with their occupants, have been examined by earth governments.

Another terrestrial hypothesis for the nature of the flying saucer phenomenon was proposed by Trevor James Constable in *They Live in the Sky*. According to Constable's theory, flying saucers are actually living organisms, he calls them 'critters,' which resemble large, airborne amoeba. These critters appear when they change their density and become visible to the human eye. Most of the time they remain invisible. Their means of propulsion is identified as 'orgonic energy,' a force common to all living things. The critters appear more frequently in recent times because of the growing use of radar, which is obviously disturbing to them. These critters are predatory and sometimes attack domesticated animals and even humans. These attacks account for unexplained disappearances as well as mutilated animal carcasses.

The 1960s saw the articulation of another theory postulating an earthly origin for flying saucers, explained by Raymond Bernard in *The Hollow Earth*. According to Bernard, flying saucers are piloted by occupants of our globe's interior who originally fled to the subterranean world at the destruction of their surface civilization of Atlantis.

> Prior to the catastrophe that destroyed Atlantis, the Atlanteans found refuge in the Subterranean World in the hollow interior of the earth, to which they traveled on their 'vimanas' or flying saucers, reaching it through the polar openings. Ever since then, their flying saucers remained in the earth's interior atmosphere and were used for transportation from one point in the interior *concave world* to another, for in this world, inside the crust of the earth, a straight aerial line is the shortest distance between any two points, no matter how far apart. It was only after the Hiroshima atomic explosion that these Atlantean aircraft rose to the surface for the first time, and were known as flying saucers. . . . [T]hey came as an act of self-defense, to prevent radioactive pollution of the air they received from the outside. (Bernard, 1964: chapter 7)

UFO religion

Finally, in the 1970s Mattern Friedrich, in his book *UFOs: Nazi Secret Weapon* claimed that UFOs were actually controlled by Nazis operating from their bases in Argentina and Antarctica. According to Friedrich, the Nazis first developed saucer technology in the 1940s and escaped with it from Europe at the end of World War II. Hitler is believed to have survived the Allied victory and to have traveled with the plans by submarine to Argentina. Subsequently a saucer base was established in Antarctica. Saucers from this base were responsible for the loss of four of Admiral Byrd's planes during his South Pole expedition, having been shot down by sound cannons. The US planned to bomb the base in retaliation, but thought better of it after the saucers buzzed Washington, DC in 1952. Today, saucers often land and attempt to make converts to the Nazi cause. Their ultimate plan is to establish world-wide dominion and the Last Battalion is ready to attack and conquer when the word is given. With their saucer technology, taken either from lost ancient civilizations or from extraterrestrials, they will be unstoppable.

Most UFO believers, however, have not been willing to accept the US or Soviet militaries, Etherians, flying critters, subterranean civilizations, or Nazis as the source of the unidentified flying objects reported around the globe. Since shortly after the first wave of sightings in the late 1940s, the extraterrestrial hypothesis has clearly been the favorite.

— Flying Saucers are Real —

One of the most influential analyses of the flying saucer phenomenon, *The Flying Saucers Are Real,* was published in 1950 by Donald E. Keyhoe. Keyhoe's was the first attempt at a systematic treatment of the flying saucer mystery offered in support of the extraterrestrial hypothesis and did much to establish that theory's primacy. Keyhoe would also establish the centrality of a government cover-up in UFO theory.

Keyhoe reports that it was in the spring of 1949 that he first began investigation of the mystery of the flying saucers as an assignment for *True* magazine. At that time he was skeptical of the veracity of the reports, but that skepticism about UFO reports would soon give way to skepticism concerning the explanations offered by the government.

> For six months, I worked with other investigators to solve the mystery of the disks. We checked a hundred sighting reports, frequently crossing the trail of Project 'Saucer' teams and F.B.I. agents. Old records gave fantastic leads. So did Air Force plans for exploring space. Rocket experts, astronomers, Air Force officials and pilots gave us clues. (Keyhoe, 1950: 8)

The conclusions that Keyhoe reached at the end of his research were published in the January 1950 issue of *True* and formed the foundation of his subsequent book. First, Keyhoe concluded that the earth had been observed by visitors from outer space. Second, he claimed that the extent of this observation had radically increased in the preceding two years. The only other possible explanation, according to Keyhoe, is that saucers are extremely sophisticated craft developed on earth. He rules this out, however, as requiring an unbelievable leap in human technical progress.

If, as Keyhoe believes, the extraterrestrial hypothesis is the most reasonable account of the flying saucer mystery then the question arises as to why the government and the military have not reached this conclusion for themselves, and if they have reached this conclusion, why they haven't made it public. One of the most important sightings, and one directly related to the US military, is the sighting associated with the accidental death of Air Force pilot Captain Thomas Mantell. According to Keyhoe's description of the event, Captain Mantell's death on January 7, 1948 was the result of an encounter with an unidentified flying object. Army MPs at Fort Knox reported that state police had sighted a large bright object in the sky. The object had also been seen by hundreds of residents of nearby Madisonville, Kentucky. Soon after the state police report the object was seen over the military base itself. It remained stationary above the base for at least an hour. Then, P-51 aircraft, already airborne, reported that they had spotted the object as well. The flight leader, Mantell, made the initial report.

> 'I've sighted the thing!' he said. 'It looks metallic – and it's tremendous in size!'
> The C.O. and Woods stared at each other. No one spoke.

'The thing's starting to climb,' Mantell said swiftly. 'It's at twelve o'clock high, making half my speed. I'll try to close in.'

In five minutes, Mantell reported again. The strange metallic object had speeded up, was now making 360 or more.

At 3:08, Mantell's wingman called in. Both he and the other pilot had seen the weird object. But Mantell had outclimbed them and was lost in the clouds.

Seven minutes dragged by. The men in the tower sweated out the silence. Then, at 3:15, Mantell made a hasty contact.

'It's still above me, making my speed or better. I'm going up to twenty thousand feet. If I'm no closer, I'll abandon chase.'

It was his last report.

Minutes later, his fighter disintegrated with terrific force. The falling wreckage was scattered for thousands of feet. (Keyhoe, 1950: 15–16)

The response of the Air Force to this event and others investigated by its Project Saucer was less than satisfactory to Keyhoe. They claimed that the object sighted by civilian and military witnesses and by the P-51 pilots was either a weather balloon or the planet Venus. Keyhoe argues that neither of those answers fits the details of the case. Indeed, the military itself seemed to recognize the limitations of these answers for they offered a third possibility, that it was a Soviet craft. Pursuing this possibility, Keyhoe again reached the conclusion that this was not a likely scenario. All of this raised the question as to why the military would offer such implausible explanations. For Keyhoe, the answer was obvious. They offered these explanations to hide the truth.

While Keyhoe's article in *True* magazine helped to establish the extraterrestrial hypothesis as the most likely explanation for flying saucer sightings, his conclusions in *The Flying Saucers Are Real* established the theme of a government cover-up of the truth and of its plan to release information gradually in a way that would not cause public panic. This explains, according to Keyhoe, why the government itself has seemed to waver between denial and acceptance of the extraterrestrial hypothesis. By releasing bits of the truth they hoped to make the idea more palatable when it was finally told in full. In addition, Keyhoe's explanation of the saucer mystery as articulated in his book had changed somewhat from his earlier position. After becoming acquainted with the nineteenth-century airship mystery, Keyhoe reached the conclusion that the earth had been visited by extraterrestrials for at least two hundred years. He came to believe that these visitations increased greatly in 1947 on the heels of the atom bomb explosions beginning in 1945. Both of these ideas, that visitations from extraterrestrials have historical precedent and that part of the motivation for the visits must be the development of nuclear weapons, would become important elements in much ufological theory. Keyhoe also believed that this extraterrestrial observation is part of a long-range survey that may or may not result in contact with humans. If such contact is made, however, Keyhoe sounds a note that is far more optimistic than the one he attributes to the US government.

> Americans cannot escape eventual contact with dwellers on other planets. Even though space visitors never attempt contact with us, sooner or later earthlings will be traveling to distant planets – planets that scientists have said are almost surely inhabited.
> The American people have proved their ability to take incredible things. We have survived the stunning impact of the Atomic Age. We should be able to take the Interplanetary Age, when it comes, without hysteria. (Keyhoe, 1950: 175)

— Flying Saucers – Here and Now —

Some fifteen years later the same themes were re-emphasized in the best-selling books of Frank Edwards. In *Flying Saucers: Serious Business* (1966) and *Flying Saucers: Here and Now* (1967) Edwards argued that unidentified flying objects were clearly extraterrestrial in origin. He likewise followed Keyhoe to emphasize the cover-up of this fact perpetuated by the US government. The first of these claims, the extraterrestrial origin of UFOs, was explored in *Here and Now* with an account of a sixteen-month period in 1965 and 1966 when the occurrences of UFO reports were at an all-time high. According to Edwards, the intense UFO activity that occurred in 1965 and 1966 came to prominence on the night of August 2, 1965 . . .

> when an estimated quarter of a million persons stood out in the Great Plains states of the United States and watched the formations of unusual lights maneuvering overhead.

UFO religion

The things were seen with the naked eye and with a wide variety of optical instruments. They were tracked on radar, both civilian and military. They were photographed by both amateur and professional photographers. They followed planes, including a jet passenger plane piloted by a good friend of mine.

Next morning when the official explanation was handed out, assuring one and all that they had seen nothing more than four stars in the constellation Orion, my pilot friend commented wryly:

'Last night was the first time in my life that I have flown across Nebraska with three stars under my right wing.' (Edwards, 1967: 3)

Like Keyhoe fifteen years before, Edwards was amazed at what he called the 'theme of Air Force misinformation and ineptitude' that followed this sighting and others. This misinformation and ineptitude, in Edwards's estimation, reached a climax in March, 1966 when Dr. J. Allen Hynek, consultant to the Air Force on UFO issues, claimed that the explanation of a well-documented sighting was probably 'swamp gas.' Like Keyhoe, Edwards believed that such ridiculous explanations on the part of the government and the military were clearly an attempt to disguise the real nature of the saucers, which must have been rather clearer to the government and the military than they were willing to admit.

Edwards, as a matter of fact, suggested that he had unwittingly stumbled upon the real government position already clearly articulated in 1950. That was the year that he was invited by a friend to attend a military briefing on the subject of space exploration. The briefing, much to Edwards's surprise, consisted of an elaborate and well-thought-out discussion of the US government's plan for encounters with extraterrestrial civilizations, which might occur as a part of US space exploration efforts. This seven-point plan struck Edwards at the time as being far ahead of the reality of the then nonexistent US space program. Later, he came to wonder if the government's plan was meant to lay the groundwork for a public understanding of extraterrestrial encounters in reverse, namely the exploration of earth by beings from other planets. As Edwards understood it, the seven-point plan for US space exploration was in reality the first public statement of the government's understanding of the nature and purpose of the flying saucers.

Phase One of the plan to explore other planets is the approach. This phase would have as its purpose the determination of whether or not a planet was inhabited. It would take place from a safe distance and would be completely unknown to any of the planet's potential inhabitants. Phase Two would consist of a close-up examination of the planet by unmanned probes. The purpose of the probes would be to collect photographs and soil and atmosphere samples. They would also seek to determine the existence of intelligent life and the location of the largest centers of population of any intelligent species. In Phase Three, assuming that Phase Two provided adequate reason for doing so, piloted craft would explore the planet. One of the most important features of these missions would be the determination of the scientific, technological, and military status of the indigenous culture. Phase Four would consist of near approaches to determine whether or not the culture showed signs of hostility. Phase Five would be marked by touchdowns in isolated parts of the planet to obtain specimens of the indigenous life forms, perhaps even of any intelligent species. Phase Six would take place after the decision was made to make contact. It would consist of low-level approaches that would allow the locals to see our craft and our personnel but not harm them or reach them in any way. This phase would thus allow the indigenous population to know of our existence and to know that our intentions were peaceful. Phase Seven

> would be the deliberate, carefully planned and executed final step in the program. Contact would not be attempted unless we had excellent reason to believe that it would not be disastrous to either of the races involved. There are many reasons why this final step might never come to pass – even though results of the first six phases might have indicated that it could be physically possible. (Edwards, 1967: 40–1)

According to Edwards, the military knows the truth behind the flying saucers and would like to share that information with the public. However, this information could not be provided directly for fear that the public would respond with panic. The solution was to introduce the general idea of extraterrestrial contact to the public without explicitly informing them that such contact was currently underway on earth. Once again, with Edwards as with Keyhoe, the extraterrestrial hypothesis was accompanied by the theme of government cover-up. Keyhoe and Edwards were so convinced of the obviousness of the extraterrestrial hypothesis that they could not accept that the government would not have come to that conclusion as well. The answer must be that the government knows the truth about the extraterrestrial origin of UFOs but is afraid to make that knowledge public for fear of panic. What is interesting about their way of thinking is the amount of confidence they both seem to have in the government, despite the cover-up. The government is neither inept nor malicious. It is certainly smart enough to have come to the truth of the extraterrestrial hypothesis on its own and its attempt to keep this from the public is meant for public good. While the first of these attitudes toward the government is maintained in most subsequent saucer theories, the second of these, as we shall see more clearly in later chapters, has not been nearly so long lived. For now, however, we turn our attention to a third important saucer theorist, this one with a view from inside the governmental/military establishment.

— Close Encounters —

Former analyst and spokesperson for the Air Force's Project Blue Book, J. Allen Hynek was one of those singled out for criticism by Frank Edwards, especially for Hynek's statement that a particular sighting might best be explained as 'swamp gas.' However, by the time of the publication of his book *The UFO Experience: A Scientific Inquiry* (1972), Hynek, having broken with the Air Force over what he regarded as a refusal to consider the evidence in a true scientific fashion, was recognized as a defender of the extraterrestrial origin of saucers as at least one viable hypothesis in need of consideration. As a former insider Hynek had less confidence in the government's abilities than did other theorists and saw, not a cover-up, but a true refusal on the government's part to accept the logical conclusion to the saucer mystery. Hynek's strategy was to provide something the military would not accept, a scientific inquiry into the UFO experience. The result is a phenomenological analysis of the kinds of experiences that people claim to have had.

First, Hynek describes the most common type of UFO experience, what he calls *Nocturnal Lights*. Providing several examples of nocturnal light sightings, Hynek summarizes them in this way:

> The typical Nocturnal Light is a bright light, generally not a point source, of indeterminate linear size and of varying color but most usually yellowish orange, although no color of the spectrum has been consistently absent, which follows a path not ascribable to a balloon, aircraft, or other natural object and which often gives the appearance of intelligent action. The light gives no direct evidence of being attached to a solid body but presumably may be. (Hynek, 1972: 56)

The second category of UFO experience is what Hynek calls the *Daylight Disc* experience. Again, after providing several examples of daylight sightings, Hynek provides a summary description:

> [T]he object (often objects in pairs) is variously described as oval, disc shaped, 'a stunted dill pickle,' and ellipsoid. It generally is shiny or glowing (but almost never described as having distinct point source lights), yellowish, white, or metallic. It exhibits in most cases what we would anthropomorphically describe as 'purposeful' directed motion, with the ability to accelerate extremely rapidly. No loud sounds or roars seem to be associated with the Daylight Discs; sometimes there is a faint swishing sound. (Hynek, 1972: 76–7)

The third category consists of unexplained *Radar Visual Reports*, some accompanied by visual observer experiences as well.

The most important type of UFO experience, however, is what Hynek calls the *Close Encounter*, of which he identifies three types. Close Encounters are defined as sightings of lights or objects close to the observers, less than 500 feet away. *Close Encounters of the First Kind* consist of reports of near sightings unaccompanied by any tangible effects. *Close Encounters of the Second Kind* are near sightings accompanied by measurable effects on either animate or inanimate objects, usually including such things as landing marks in the soil or physical burns or marks on the observers. Finally, *Close Encounters of the Third Kind* consist of near reports that include sightings of the craft's occupants (Hynek, 1972: 98–9) Hynek's classification system became famous with the release of Steven Spielburg's movie *Close Encounters of the Third Kind*, for which Hynek served as a consultant and in which he appeared in a brief cameo.

UFO religion

Hynek provides examples of all three types of Close Encounters. The following is a typical example of a Close Encounter involving occupants of the saucer:

> This case had four witnesses, all family men holding responsible positions. Two are engaged in work requiring military clearance, and their jobs would be in severe jeopardy were their anonymity violated. For the record, this reported event took place in North Dakota in November, 1961, in rain and sleet, late at night. The four men observed the landing of a lighted craft in a completely open and deserted field and, thinking that an aircraft was in serious trouble, stopped by the roadside, hopped the fence, and hurried toward what they judged to be the plane. Their surprise was understandably great when they discovered humanoids around the craft, one of which boldly waved them off in a threatening manner. One of the men fired a shot at the humanoid, which fell as if hurt. The craft soon took off, and the men fled. (Hynek, 1972: 164)

Hynek's conclusion is not that the sighting reports point inevitably to the extraterrestrial hypothesis but rather that they demand the kind of careful study that the Air Force and the US government had refused to give them. His categorization of the different types of sightings provides no answer to the mystery, but rather a description of what is in need of explanation:

> the localization of the phenomenon in space and time, its apparently intelligent characteristics (of a rather puerile kind), its appearance of operating outside the established laws of physics, and its peculiar preferences for certain situations. The frequently reported presence of 'humanoids' capable of moving about in comfort in our highly restrictive terrestrial environment, and their association with 'craft,' exhibiting at times near-zero inertial mass yet able to leave physical traces of its presence . . . (Hynek, 1972: 262)

It may be, argued Hynek, that an explanation of the phenomena that he has described is outside the pale of contemporary science and must wait for future paradigms of investigation and understanding. If this is the case, the duty of contemporary science is not to dismiss the phenomena, but to carefully record and document sightings in the hope of a future solution.

[T]here will surely be, we hope, a twenty-first century science and a thirtieth century science, and perhaps they will encompass the UFO phenomenon as twentieth century science has encompassed the aurora borealis, a feat unimaginable to nineteenth century science, which likewise was incapable of explaining how the sun and stars shine. (Hynek, 1972: 262)

◆ ◆ ◆

Even upon their arrival in the Mojave at the designated sky watch gathering place, I was ignorant of my companions' identities. The pitch-black darkness made it impossible for me to make out any features. They were just shadows and disembodied voices. Following the beam of a flashlight held by the person in front of me, I made my way down from the parking area to a spot of open desert, bounded on three sides by scrub and on the fourth by the rock-strewn hillside we had just descended. A blanket was spread on the desert sand and after a hesitant moment trying to decide how to go about this, we finally all lay on our backs, heads touching in a way that enabled us to see the sky above in all directions.

Despite the growing cold it was not long before my uneasiness with my situation completely slipped away. The people gathered here on this darkest of nights seemed to know no more about how to go about this than I did. After a few moments of staring uneventfully into the starry night someone suggested lighting a flare in hopes of attracting 'their' attention. After it was pointed out that we had come to the desert to get away from the lights of the city, and that if we lit a flare we would not be able to see anything, he acquiesced to our wishes and we remained in the dark. A few moments later someone asked for a joint, suggesting that it might improve our ability to make mental contact with extraterrestrials. After a brief discussion it was discovered that no one had come so prepared. Two of our company moved to the outer part of our circle and began playing didgeridoos (is that the plural?). Was this supposed to attract them? Were the ETs from Australia? It didn't matter. This was cool and not nearly so scary as the aurora borealis. No sightings mind you, unless you count my faceless friends, but no sightings needed. The stars still and constant; didgeridoos playing eerily in the darkness; faceless and nameless humans staring infinity in the eye; nothing to see but stars and sand; the conversation reflective and quiet. No fear here, only wonder, expectation, awe. 'I saw the saucers hover over Washington in 1952.' 'I was awakened in the night by the visitors.' 'I have not seen them, but I want to, am trying to, would love to.' 'Is that a star or an airplane, or . . .?' 'What if they are watching us from behind the brush?' Strangers in the desert, drawn like moths to a flame, no, not to a flame, to the darkness; no aurora borealis, only black sky dotted with stars; that same sense of awe only without the sick to my stomach terror; that same sense of wonder. I'm like a kid again, for once as an adult not certain what is going to happen next, for once not caring that events were out of my control, for once hoping to be surprised, shocked, even terrorized.

While Keyhoe and Edwards believed that the military/government establishment must already have the answer to the saucer mystery, Hynek could only hope that science would solve the mystery in the future, just as it has solved so many mysteries in the past. He hoped that UFOs would one day be explained by science just as science has explained star-shine and the aurora borealis. Keyhoe, Edwards, and Hynek argued that flying saucers are real, here and now, and that experiences with UFOs need to be counted and cataloged, analyzed and categorized. They were clearly proponents of 'nuts and bolts' ufology. Flying saucers, according to their approach, are physical objects, held together, we suppose, by nuts and bolts, powered by physical forces, inhabited by physical beings. The solution to the mystery of the saucers will require the careful cataloging of the physical details of the experiences. I, however, cannot help but feel that this approach, in a way, misses the point. They are talking about solving a mystery. That is different from experiencing the mysterious. To know the cause of the aurora borealis or a star's shine in no way takes away their power, at certain times and in certain places, in childhood epiphanies and the desert darkness, to overwhelm us with wonder.

This isn't the end of the nuts and bolts, however, for where there are nuts and bolts there are bound to be loose screws, and when you have loose screws things can sometimes go terribly wrong.

2

Crashes

2. Outside the Little A'Le'Inn, Rachel, Nevada

— Aurora —

On April 17, 1897 the famous airship that had been reported cruising above California, the Midwest, and Texas made a startling appearance in the *Dallas Morning News*. According to S. E. Haydon, cotton merchant and part-time *News* correspondent, the airship had been spotted in the skies above Aurora, Texas at around six o'clock that morning. It was traveling north at a much lower altitude than was usual. Haydon reported:

> Evidently some of the machinery was out of order, for it was making a speed of only ten or twelve miles an hour, and gradually settling toward the earth. It sailed over the public square and when it reached the north part of town it collided with the tower of Judge Proctor's windmill and went into pieces with a terrific explosion, scattering debris over several acres of ground, wrecking the windmill and water tank and destroying the judge's flower garden. (Chariton, 1991: 198)

The only inhabitant of the crashed airship was deceased, his body very badly burned and disfigured. However, it was clear that the crewman was not from this world. A Mr. T. J. Weems, US Signal Service officer, expressed his conviction that Mars was his place of origin. There were papers found on his person, written in a type of hieroglyphics that no one was able to decipher. The craft itself was too damaged to be examined in any detail, though it was reported that it seemed to be a mixture of aluminum and silver and weighed several tons. Townspeople gathered to view the wreck and collect souvenirs of the strange metal. It was announced that a funeral for the pilot would be held on the following day.

Remarkably, this report appeared tucked away on page five of the newspaper. One would think that if the newspaper had meant this for more than entertainment it would have appeared under a banner headline on page one and have been carried in newspapers around the world. As it was, the *Fort Worth Register* appears to have been the only other newspaper to carry the story. Neither the *News* nor the *Register* bothered to send a reporter to Aurora, just a short distance north of Dallas and Fort Worth, to attend the spaceman's funeral, supposedly scheduled for the next day. There were also no reports of the funeral in any local obituaries.

This story was mostly forgotten until Frank Tolbert, columnist for the *Dallas Morning News*, revived it in the mid-1960s after a reader sent him a copy of the original story. This was, of course, right in the middle of the UFO heyday and ufologists jumped on the idea that a saucer might have crashed in Texas in the late nineteenth century. Saucer investigators descended on the town, including a well-publicized 1973 team sponsored by the Mutual UFO Network. The 1973 version of the story turned out to gain far more publicity than the original story ever had. Investigators managed to unearth witnesses willing to testify that they remembered hearing about the saucer crash from loved ones who had seen it in person, and while second-person accounts may not sound all that spectacular, they were not the only things to be unearthed.

Within the confines of the Aurora Cemetery some of the investigators thought they might have located the grave of the extraterrestrial. An old grave with a crude sandstone marker was the focus of much attention. Upon the marker was a triangle with three small circles inside. While many people argued that the markings looked like nothing more than arbitrary features of the stone, others were convinced that they were meant to represent the airship that had crashed so many years before. To make the idea even more enticing, metal detectors found indications of metal within the gravesite. Investigators requested permission to exhume the body. Much to their disappointment, the request was denied (Chariton, 1991: 205–6).

Then, sometime between midnight and dawn on June 14, 1973 the spaceman's tombstone was stolen from the Aurora cemetery. In addition, it was reported in the July 4, 1973 *Dallas Times Herald* that the robbers had used long metal probes to explore the grave, perhaps collecting metallic specimens or samples from the body. The whereabouts of the stone and the results of any analysis performed on the specimens remain unknown (Cohen, 1981: 103).

Surprisingly enough, the Aurora crash story was not the first of its kind. As far as I can tell that distinction goes to an 1884 story found in the *Nebraska Nugget* of Holdrege, Nebraska. According to this report, on June 6, 1884 rancher John Ellis and three of his herdsmen were involved in a round-up when they heard a loud noise from above. Looking up they saw a flaming object crash to the earth. Riding to the crash site, the men saw cog-wheels and other pieces of machinery on the ground. The machinery was red hot, scorching the ground wherever it lay. The article described the scene in this way:

> The heat from this strange wreck was so intense that a cowboy named Williamson fell senseless from gazing at it at too close quarters. His face was blistered, and his hair singed to a crisp. His condition is said to be dangerous. ... Finding it impossible to approach the mysterious visitor, the party turned back on its trail. When it first touched the earth the ground was sandy and

bare of grass. The sand was fused to an unknown depth over a space of about 20 feet wide by 30 feet long, and the melted stuff was bubbling and hissing.

Once the objects cooled it did become possible to examine them more carefully:

> One piece that looked like the blade of a propeller screw, of metal in appearance like brass, about 16 inches wide, 3 inches thick, and 3½ feet long, was picked up on a spade. It would not weigh more than five pounds, but appeared as strong and compact as any metal. A fragment of a wheel with a milled rim, apparently having a diameter of seven or eight feet, was also picked up. It seemed to be of the same material and had the same remarkable lightness. The aerolite, or whatever it is, seems to be about 50 or 60 feet long, cylindrical, and about 10 or 12 feet in diameter. (Cohen, 1981: 170)

There may have been other similar newspaper accounts, lost now to history. They, like the Aurora crash and the story from the *Nugget* should probably be regarded as newspaper hoaxes. What is important to see is that long before the UFO craze of the 1950s and 1960s, and long before the supposed 1947 crash at Roswell, crashed spaceships and deceased extraterrestrials were already a part of the burgeoning popular culture. Though neither of these crash stories necessarily had any direct influence on the more famous crash stories of the twentieth century – indeed it was the crash stories of the twentieth century that brought these nineteenth-century tales back from obscurity – they do provide a glimmer of things that were to come.

The Aurora story in particular has almost every element of a good twentieth-century saucer crash, from the dead extraterrestrial found on board to the strange hieroglyphic writings. It differs in that it takes place in the middle of town, right there in Aurora, its flames lighting up the sky like those famed northern lights. It was observed by the whole town, everyone gathered to watch the spectacle or to claim a piece of the vessel as their own. The spaceman was given what one supposes was a 'proper Christian burial' and then laid to rest in the Aurora cemetery, probably called then what we called cemeteries when I was growing up – graveyards. Everyone saw it, and if you don't believe, just take a look in the graveyard. This is, of course, a far cry from what the twentieth century would bring, at Roswell and at the less well-known Aztec. In those stories the saucers would crash in the desert, away from eyewitnesses. The wreckage, though handled by plenty of witnesses, was collected by the government for safe keeping. And there would have been no Christian burials for those ETs, no spot in the graveyard under an old and knotted cedar tree. No, those bodies would be spirited away, autopsied, kept under lock and key, preserved in formaldehyde, to be brought out every now and again for inspection. Much would be similar, between Aurora and Aztec, but those things would be completely changed.

— Aztec —

In 1950 Frank Scully, a well-known entertainment writer for *Variety* and the namesake of *The X-Files* character, published *Behind the Flying Saucers*. In this book Scully claimed to have knowledge of crashed flying saucers that had been recovered by the US government from the deserts of the American Southwest. The story proffered by Scully appeared on the surface quite complicated, a fact that was not helped by Scully's non-linear approach to story telling and his attempt to explain the operations of the saucers through the theory of what he called magnetic lines of force. As Scully described it:

> When the Earth shifts a fraction there is a magnetic disturbance around the poles and that's all the Aurora Borealis is. These magnetic lines of force go as deep as the skin of the Earth, which is 32 miles. It is assumed that the Sun supplies its other planets with this energy as it does us. It is assumed that they are all positive forces and thus repel each other and so keep in magnetic balance. Anybody who can effect a negative current can get from one positive planet to another positive planet. (Scully, 1950: 167)

At its core Scully's story is a rather straightforward account of the crash and recovery of not one but three extraterrestrial spacecraft.

Though not appearing until well over half-way through his book, Scully's crash recovery story begins . . .

UFO religion

> In the summer of 1949, while consorting with men engaged in magnetic research on the Mojave Desert, I met a man of science whose contemporaries rated him the top magnetic research specialist in the United States. He had more degrees than a thermometer and had received them from such diverse institutions as Armour Institute, Creighton University, and the University of Berlin. He is the scientist I have called Dr. Gee. (Scully, 1950: 127)

In addition to having 'more degrees than a thermometer,' Dr. Gee had been involved in top-secret research during World War II that focused on the use of magnetism in offensive strikes against enemy aircraft. The research was so top secret that the existence of the program had never been publicized, except of course until revealed by Scully. Unlike many other scientists who worked on the war effort, Dr. Gee remained in the service of the military after the war came to an end. It was in that capacity that Dr. Gee had been called in to help in the analysis of the crashed saucers. I can't resist quoting from Scully on this point. You'll see why . . .

> He was the man who told us the whole story of the first flying saucer that had landed in the United States. Another had landed in the Sahara before this, but that one was more cracked than a psychiatrist in an auto wreck. But the one he had worked on had gently pancaked to earth like a slow motion of Sonja Henie imitating a dying swan. (Scully, 1950: 128)

(See, I told you. You just don't read prose like that everyday.) The craft had been observed as it descended into the atmosphere and the Air Force had quickly been scrambled to respond. Within hours the craft was cordoned off and Dr. Gee and his merry band of magnetic investigators had been called in to examine it.

For two days the scientists avoided direct contact with the craft and instead examined it through every long-distance means at their disposal, as Scully put it, 'bombing it with Geiger counters, cosmic rays, and other protective devices' (1950: 128), whatever that means. Finally comfortable with a closer approach, the team faced the dilemma of how to get inside the vehicle. The only possibility seemed to be a broken porthole that, according to Dr. Gee, appeared on first examination to be made of glass. However, he reported that 'On closer examination we found it was a good deal different from any glass in this country' (Scully, 1950: 129). How did the scientists approach the challenge of investigating the craft through the crack in this 'un-American' glass porthole? Dr. Gee explains, 'Finally, we took a large pole and rammed a hole through this defect in the ship' (Scully, 1950: 129). Of course, just what I would have done.

Looking inside, the team discovered the presence of sixteen bodies, ranging in height from 36 to 42 inches. Fortunately, when the pole was shoved through the broken porthole it happened to hit a knob on the opposite wall, which opened a door. According to Dr. Gee:

> This enabled us to get into the ship.
> We took the little bodies out, and laid them on the ground. We examined them and their clothing. I remember one of our team saying, 'That looks the style of 1890.' We examined the bodies very closely and very carefully. They were normal from every standpoint and had no appearance of being what we call on this planet 'midgets.' They were perfectly normal in their development. The only trouble was that their skin seemed to be charred a very dark chocolate color. (Scully, 1950: 129)

Confirming the many sightings of UFOs that had taken place in the last few years, Dr. Gee described the craft as looking like a huge saucer, though he adds an important detail to this description, saying 'you might almost say that there was a cup in [the saucer], because the cabin set in an insert in the bottom of a saucer' (Scully, 1950: 130). Thus would a more accurate description than 'flying saucer' seem to be 'flying cup and saucer'?

Once inside the vessel, the team of crack scientists was unsure what to do, though Dr. Gee was the first to suggest that it was propelled by 'magnetic lines of force.' Other than that suggestion, however, the team seems to have been stumped.

> Some of [Dr. Gee's] staff suggested pushing some of the buttons on what appeared to be the instrument board to find out if his suspicions were true. But all agreed after some discussion that that would be about the worst possible thing they could do, because if the ship started, nobody would know which button to push to stop it again.
> 'So the result was,' said Dr Gee, 'that none of us pushed any buttons on the instrument board.' (Scully, 1950: 130)

Two crewmen were found slumped over the instrument panel, having fallen out of what Scully describes as 'bucket seats' (1950: 130). (Tiny bucket seats, I suppose.) Dr. Gee also reported the discovery of 'pamphlets' that he suspected dealt with navigation problems. The writing was indecipherable, though it looked like a pictorial script, reminiscent of Egyptian hieroglyphics. As this was the case, I suppose they might just as well have been pamphlets warning of the dangers of sexually transmitted diseases when in contact with alien life forms.

The craft was subsequently, and much to Dr. Gee's disapproval, broken down and transported to a government testing laboratory. The crew of the ship was treated very differently to the lone spaceman in Aurora. Dr. Gee reported that they had been dissected by the medical division of the Air Force. The meager reports he had acquired subsequently indicated that his first impression had been correct. Despite their diminutive size, the spacemen were in every detail identical to earth humans, with the exception of their teeth, which were completely without cavities and perfect in every way. They were judged to be between thirty-five and forty years of age. Venus was suggested as the most likely point of origin for the ship, due to the diminutive size of the occupants.

Other details were equally interesting. Their uniforms showed no signs of insignia or other indications of rank, leading Dr. Gee to suppose that theirs was a very egalitarian society. The only food discovered on the ship consisted of little wafers. These wafers were tested on guinea pigs, which seemed to thrive on the spacemen's diet. Furthermore, 'On one occasion one wafer was put into a gallon container of boiling water and it very quickly boiled over the sides of the container' (Scully, 1950: 134). Interesting.

Later in his conversations with Dr. Gee, Scully learned that there were three saucers in the possession of the Air Force; the other two craft had landed in Arizona. A fourth had 'got away' (Scully, 1950: 135). The second craft was in similar condition to the first, except that the door was already open and the sixteen crewmembers, though dead, were not burned. Dr. Gee speculated that they died when the craft was contaminated by our atmosphere. When the third craft was discovered one of the little men was found dead, half-way out of the escape hatch. The only other crewmember of this much smaller craft was dead at the control board.

The bigger craft came equipped with sleeping quarters:

> Pushed back into the wall was what turned out to be a collapsible or accordion type screen, and as it was pulled out, it moved around in a half circle, so that by the time it reached the wall of the circular cabin little hammocks had dropped down from this screen or accordion-like wall, and there were the sleeping quarters for these men.
>
> He said there were toilet facilities inside the sleeping quarters. The smallest ship, however, had no such conveniences, from which the doctor deduced they were making round trips so fast they didn't feel the need of such facilities. (Scully, 1950: 136)

Of course, none of this would ever be officially admitted by the Air Force or the US government. The 'Pentagonians,' as Scully calls the top military brass, were too embarrassed that they missed the boat on magnetic power, focusing all of their energies on jet propulsion. According to Dr. Gee, current earth technology is at least 500 years behind the aliens, at least as far as interstellar flights and magnetic propulsion is concerned. The fact that the US military placed all of its hopes on the wrong technology, bet on the wrong horse, is a fact they cannot stand to have revealed. Consequently, according to Scully, the claims of Dr. Gee would have to stand without official confirmation from the government or the academic researchers who receive their financial support from the government.

Behind the Flying Saucers was a bestseller and for a short while seemed to offer strong support to the extraterrestrial hypothesis. The Scully book was not to stand up under scrutiny, however, and its influence, though still important, would be mostly indirect. The fall of Scully's story of the Aztec crash was noted in the pages of *True* magazine, the magazine that, in articles by Donald Keyhoe, had been an early champion of the extraterrestrial hypothesis. In two articles written by J. P. Cahn, the Aztec crash was shown conclusively to have been a hoax perpetrated by Dr. Gee and his partner Silas Newton in an attempt to encourage interest in equipment that they claimed used magnetism to locate underground oil wells. In the September 1952 issue of *True*, Cahn revealed that Dr. Gee, the man with more degrees than a thermometer, was in reality Leo A.

GeBauer, local hardware store owner from Phoenix, Arizona, not the head of a secret government scientific task force charged with the study of the power of magnetism. After showing many of the claims made in the Scully book about the credentials of Newton and 'Dr. Gee' to be faulty, the clincher came when Cahn was able to surreptitiously acquire an object that Newton claimed to be a specimen from the craft. Newton also claimed that the material had been shown through extensive laboratory testing to be extraterrestrial in origin. Cahn's analysis of the material told a different story. The material, which Newton claimed could stand up to temperatures of 10,000 degrees, melted quite nicely at 657 degrees Fahrenheit. It was nothing more than good old terrestrial aluminum.

In a follow-up story Cahn reported that both Newton and GeBauer had been convicted of fraud. Apparently the crashed saucer story had generated enough interest in magnetic lines of force to convince some people to invest in the equipment that the men claimed was capable of locating underground oil. In court their inventions were shown to be empty boxes, empty that is except for the lone battery that powered one solitary flashing light. Scully, Cahn reports, was never charged with any crime and does not appear to have profited from any of the fraudulent deals, unless, of course, one considers the profits from his book. In any event, the Aztec saucer crash was revealed to be a hoax, much like the saucer crash stories of the nineteenth century, except in this case it is clear that the hoax was perpetrated in an attempt to defraud individuals of their money. Cahn's article put the Aztec crash to rest and most ufologists accepted his verdict. The Aztec story did not provide proof of the extraterrestrial hypothesis. It did, however, continue and reinforce the themes already present in saucer crash mythology. Aztec, like Aurora, came equipped with a crashed vessel, a deceased crew (burned to a crisp), hieroglyphic writing, and fragments of the vessel claimed to be evidence of its extraterrestrial origins. Also, like Aurora, the Aztec story would lie dormant for years before being revived.

In the case of Aurora that revival consisted of an attempt to exhume the remains of a supposed extraterrestrial visitor. In the case of Aztec it consists of the Aztec UFO Symposium, held annually, and serving to both spread the story of the Aztec crash and to encourage tourists to notice the little town of Aztec. Not yet having managed to catch the attention or the imagination of saucerians world-wide, Aztec surely hopes that one day they may be as famous in ufological and pop culture circles as their sister New Mexican town of Roswell.

— Roswell —

The best-known of the saucer crash stories is undoubtedly that of the crash near Roswell, New Mexico. The Roswell incident first came to national attention on July 8, 1947 when the *Roswell Daily Record* published a story that would be repeated in newspapers around the world. The story read as follows:

> The intelligence office of the 509th Bombardment group at Roswell Army Air Field announced at noon today, that the field has come into possession of a flying saucer.
>
> According to information released by the department, over authority of Maj. J. A. Marcel, intelligence officer, the disk was recovered on a ranch in the Roswell vicinity, after an unidentified rancher had notified Sheriff Geo. Wilcox, here, that he had found the instrument on his premises.
>
> Major Marcel and a detail from his department went to the ranch and recovered the disk, it was stated.
>
> After the intelligence officer here had inspected the instrument it was flown to higher headquarters.
>
> The intelligence office stated that no details of the saucer's construction or its appearance had been revealed.
>
> Mr. and Mrs. Dan Wilmot apparently were the only persons in Roswell who saw what they thought was a flying disk.
>
> They were sitting on their porch at 105 South Penn. last Wednesday night at about ten o'clock when a large glowing object zoomed out of the sky from the southeast, going in a northwesterly direction at a high rate of speed.
>
> Wilmot called Mrs. Wilmot's attention to it and both ran down into the yard to watch. It was in sight less then a minute, perhaps 40 or 50 seconds, Wilmot estimated.
>
> Wilmot said that it appeared to him to be about 1,500 feet high and going fast. He estimated between 400 and 500 miles per hour.

In appearance it looked oval in shape like two inverted saucers, faced mouth to mouth, or like two old type washbowls placed together in the same fashion. The entire body glowed as though light were showing through from inside, though not like it would be if a light were merely underneath.

From where he stood Wilmot said that the object looked to be about 5 feet in size, and making allowance for the distance it was from town he figured that it must have been 15 to 20 feet in diameter, though this was just a guess.

Wilmot said that he heard no sound but that Mrs. Wilmot said she heard a swishing sound for a very short time.

The object came into view from the southeast and disappeared over the treetops in the general vicinity of six mile hill.

Wilmot, who is one of the most respected and reliable citizens in town, kept the story to himself hoping that someone else would come out and tell about having seen one, but finally today decided that he would go ahead and tell about it. The announcement that the RAAF was in possession of one came only a few minutes after he decided to release the details of what he had seen.

To put the story into context it should be noted that Kenneth Arnold's sighting of flying saucers had just made national news when the Roswell story was written. This is important for two reasons. First, the Roswell incident occurred when the nation was in the grip of the first flying saucer flap. Second, at that time the extraterrestrial hypothesis was not considered as valid as other more terrestrial-based explanations for the origins of the sightings. One should not assume, therefore, that the incident reported in this story was meant to indicate the discovery of anything extraterrestrial. The concept of 'flying saucer' had a much vaguer application on July 8, 1947 than it does today. It would have simply indicated that the Roswell Army Air Base had come into possession of some sort of aircraft or missile. The news report of the following day, indicating that the Army had managed to identify the object as a weather balloon with accompanying radar targets was probably regarded as a fairly reasonable explanation, therefore. The rancher who had found the wreckage, W. W. Brazel, had his own version of the story – also reported in the newspaper – which served to support this mundane interpretation of the wreckage.

W. W. Brazel, 48, Lincoln county rancher living 30 miles south of Corona, today told his story of finding what the army at first described as a flying disk, but the publicity which attended his find caused him to add that if he ever found anything else short of a bomb, he sure wasn't going to say anything about it.

Brazel was brought here late yesterday by W. E. Whitmore, of radio station KGFL, had his picture taken and gave an interview to the Record and Jason Kellahin, sent here from the Albuquerque bureau of the Associated Press to cover the story. The picture he posed for was sent out over AP telephoto wire sending machine specially set up in the Record office by R. D. Adair, AP wire chief sent here from Albuquerque for the sole purpose of getting out his picture and that of sheriff George Wilcox, to whom Brazel originally gave the information of his find.

Brazel related that on June 14 he and an 8-year-old son, Vernon, were about 7 or 8 miles from the ranch house of the J. B. Foster ranch, which he operates, when they came upon a large area of bright wreckage made up of rubber strips, tinfoil, a rather tough paper and sticks.

At the time Brazel was in a hurry to get his round made and he did not pay much attention to it. But he did remark about what he had seen and on July 4 he, his wife, Vernon and a daughter, Betty, age 14, went back to the spot and gathered up quite a bit of the debris.

The next day he first heard about the flying disks, and he wondered if what he had found might be the remnants of one of these.

Monday he came to town to sell some wool and while here he went to see sheriff George Wilcox and 'whispered kinda confidential like' that he might have found a flying disk.

Wilcox got in touch with the Roswell Army Air Field and Maj. Jesse A. Marcel and a man in plain clothes accompanied him home, where they picked up the rest of the pieces of the 'disk' and went to his home to try to reconstruct it.

According to Brazel they simply could not reconstruct it at all. They tried to make a kite out of it, but could not do that and could not find any way to put it back together so that it could fit.

Then Major Marcel brought it to Roswell and that was the last he heard of it until the story broke that he had found a flying disk.

Brazel said that he did not see it fall from the sky and did not see it before it was torn up, so he did not know the size or shape it might have been, but he thought it might have been about as large as a table top. The balloon which held it up, if that was how it worked, must have been about 12 feet long, he felt, measuring the distance by the size of the room in which he sat. The rubber was smoky gray in color and scattered over an area about 200 yards in diameter.

When the debris was gathered up the tinfoil, paper, tape, and sticks made a bundle about three feet long and 7 or 8 inches thick, while the rubber made a bundle about 18 or 20 inches long and about 8 inches thick. In all, he estimated, the entire lot would have weighed maybe five pounds.

There was no sign of any metal in the area which might have been used for an engine and no sign of any propellers of any kind, although at least one paper fin had been glued onto some of the tinfoil.

There were no words to be found anywhere on the instrument, although there were letters on some of the parts. Considerable scotch tape and some tape with flowers printed upon it had been used in the construction.

No strings or wire were to be found but there were some eyelets in the paper to indicate that some sort of attachment may have been used.

Brazel said that he had previously found two weather observation balloons on the ranch, but that what he found this time did not in any way resemble either of these.

'I am sure that what I found was not any weather observation balloon,' he said. 'But if I find anything else besides a bomb they are going to have a hard time getting me to say anything about it.' (*Roswell Daily Record*, July 9, 1947)

Brazel's description of what he found as rubber strips, paper, sticks, and tin foil, as much as the official weather balloon explanation, served to bring an end to any excitement that might have been aroused by the story from the previous day. Though Brazel was unconvinced by the weather balloon explanation, there is no indication that he preferred to believe the material was from an extraterrestrial source. After all, there was no metal found among the materials, but the materials did include Scotch tape and tape with flowers printed on it. It is a long way from that description to an extraterrestrial flying saucer of the sort described later at Aztec, or earlier at Aurora. Consequently, the Roswell story disappeared from public consciousness.

But of course a good saucer crash story will never stay down for long and Roswell would be no exception. On the golden anniversary of the Roswell saucer story, the city of Roswell, New Mexico was treating the event as an absurd hybrid of historical fact and high camp. Toby Smith, in his book *Little Gray Men*, described the July 'Encounter '97' in Roswell as a celebration of all things extraterrestrial.

> There's no business like UFO business. The bandwagon, carnival commercialism of Encounter '97 is visible this first day up and down Roswell's Main Street. Church's Fried Chicken has a 'Best Alien Chicken in Town' sign; Tastee Freez: 'Our Food is Out of This World;' Big O Tires: 'E.T. Phone Home.' Dining establishments boast UFO margaritas, UFO burritos, UFO cookies. 'NO VACANCY' signs deck the horizon and rickety card tables residents have set up and decorated with homemade placards that resemble a kid's lemonade kiosk jumble the sidewalks. 'Alien rocks,' cries a crude banner a Roswellian has attached to a pile of gravel likely scraped from his driveway. 'Alien Slime' and 'Alien goo' indicate hand-scrawled labels on used miniature liquor bottles filled with strange looking sediment. By week's end, all will be sold. So will every jar of hand-spooned 'Mighty Martian Mustard (with a solar taste).' (Smith, 2000: 50)

Likewise, as reported by the Associated Press:

UFO Bash No Letdown, Roswell Says
40,000 Tourists 'Were Just Right'
The Associated Press

ROSWELL – The party's over in Roswell, and city officials are satisfied with their small town's image around the world as home to a UFO crash 50 years ago.

Jeanette Miller, convention and civic center director, said the New Mexico Department of Tourism estimates that more than 40,000 people milled about the town during a weeklong celebration of the Roswell Incident in 1947. Officials had hoped for 50,000, which would have doubled Roswell's population.

'I think you can't judge it as anything but a success,' Mayor Tom Jennings said Sunday afternoon. 'It was crowded everywhere, and whether it was 35, 40 or 50,000 people, it doesn't matter.'

The celebration was estimated to have brought in more than $21 million in money spent, Miller said.

'It was very important that the people who came here got what they needed, and I think they did. The numbers were just right,' she said.

Other than some heavy traffic, Jennings and Miller said there weren't any problems.

The event began Tuesday and ended Sunday evening.

'It's been very beneficial for the local economy, the cottage industry, and the state,' Jennings said. 'Tourists don't just stay here, they go to Santa Fe and Taos and the Carlsbad Caverns. A lot of other communities are going to benefit.'

'There's nothing wrong with capitalizing on this. Three years ago Roswell had virtually no name recognition,' Jennings said.

He said visitors and media members have been very positive about their trip to Roswell for the celebration, which included parades and products, as well as lectures and research presentations.

'I've talked with media and people from all over the world, from Paris, London, Frankfurt, Tokyo, New York and Albuquerque, and they went away with a positive image of us,' Jennings said.

'When they leave here, we want people to know more about ETs, the Roswell Incident and UFOs, but we also want them to have a good feeling about Roswell.

That and a little sunburn.' (*Albuquerque Journal*, July 7, 1997)

The success of Roswell Experience '97 as well as the many television programs, movies, and books that deal with the Roswell incident cannot really be traced to those original newspaper stories of 1947, those stories of weather balloons, Scotch tape, and tin foil. For thirty years the Roswell story lay dormant. As time passed, Frank Scully published his book about Aztec, which had more in common with Aurora than with Roswell; science-fiction films established an indelible image of flying saucers and their alien occupants; and the Watergate scandal and the Vietnam War made Americans even more suspicious of their government than they had been at the time of Scully's book. No, the impetus for all of the hoopla about Roswell dates not to 1947 but rather to the late 1970s and early 1980s, to a time after the Scully hoax and after the revival of the Aurora story. When Roswell came back it came back with the elements of saucer crash mythology solidly attached. At Roswell, finally, as at Aurora and Aztec, there would be alien bodies, hieroglyphic writing, and saucer fragments. Of course the original Roswell story supplied a base for the latter two elements. The early stories had reported the discovery of wreckage – tin foil and Scotch tape though

it might have been – and they had reported that some of the fragments had letters printed on them, and that some of the tape seemed
to have pictures of flowers. Tin foil, Scotch tape and flowers: that
would be enough to turn Roswell into the biggest saucer crash story
of them all.

Though the revived story would be expanded upon by subsequent authors like Don Berliner and Stanton T. Friedman in *Crash at
Corona* (1992) and Kevin D. Randle and Donald R. Schmitt in *UFO
Crash at Roswell* (1991), the first popular retelling of the story that
would establish all of the major elements of the tale was published
by Charles Berlitz and William Moore as *The Roswell Incident* (1980).
In *The Roswell Incident*, Berlitz and Moore presented a retelling of the
Roswell saucer story with expanded roles for the wreckage fragments and the hieroglyphic lettering. They would also tell the story
to include, of course, a dead extraterrestrial crew. An indication of
how the story would be told in their hands is found in their recount-
ing of the 'original' Roswell story.

> Events which had been reported in the press and by radio before
> security regulations were imposed by the Army Air Force
> (whose name was changed to the Air Force in that very year,
> 1947) indicate that the material from the wrecked UFO was
> shuttled by high-security government transportation from base
> to base and that the remains of the UFO and the dead occupants
> (one of whom was reportedly alive when found) are under high-
> security guard at CIA headquarters at Langley, Virginia.

Likewise,

> The sketchy information used by Lieutenant Haut to write his
> initial news release was hardly sufficient to supply the press with
> certain additional details of possibly crucial importance which
> numerous other witnesses, including ranchers, soldiers, a civil
> engineer, a group of student archaeologists, and law enforce-
> ment officers, had observed at two distinctly different sites
> within the area that were apparently connected with the same
> crash. These reputedly included a large flying saucer and the
> remains of half a dozen or so humanoid creatures, pale in skin
> coloring, about four feet tall, and dressed in a kind of one-piece
> jump-suit uniform. Nor did they mention a great quantity of
> highly unusual wreckage, much of it metallic in nature, appar-
> ently originating from the same object and described by Major

Marcel as 'nothing made on this earth.' Neither was any mention made to the press of later information reported by witnesses, concerning certain columns of hieroglyphic-like writing or recording on a wooden-like substance (that was not wood) and similar unknown lettering on the control panels of the disc or saucer. (Berlitz and Moore, 1980: 2 and 30)

Moore and Berlitz weave together details from the 1947 Roswell crashed saucer story with additional details from the crashed saucer lore that that was common to both the Aurora and Aztec accounts. Indeed, their indebtedness to Scully's account of Aztec is noted quite explicitly. Scully, they argue, had many of the details of the saucer crash correct. His mistake was to identify the location as Aztec rather than Roswell. Because he rushed the story into print, he published mistakes that would have been remedied by additional research. Nevertheless, Scully's account of the Aztec crash may be used as a source for the Roswell crash.

Add to this mix the additional and recent testimony of second-generation witnesses, including the children of the story's principal participants, and the Roswell story becomes even more detailed. While these accounts often sound similar, if not identical, to those published in the original Roswell newspaper accounts, Moore and Berlitz interpret them through the lens of Scully's Aztec story. For example, Jesse Marcel Jr. described the wreckage in the following way:

> There were all kinds of stuff – small beams about three eighths or a half inch square with some sort of hieroglyphics on them that nobody could decipher. They looked something like balsa wood, and were of about the same weight, except that they were not wood at all. They were very hard, although flexible, and would not burn. There was a great deal of unusual parchment-like substance which was brown in color and extremely strong, and a great number of small pieces of a metal like tinfoil, except that it wasn't tinfoil.

Similarly, his sister described the wreckage as consisting of paper, aluminum foil, and tape, and as being distinguished by hieroglyphic writing or pastel flowers or designs:

> There was what appeared to be pieces of heavily waxed paper and a sort of aluminum like foil. Some of these pieces had some-

thing like numbers and lettering on them, but there were no words that we were able to make out. Some of the metal-foil pieces had a sort of tape stuck to them, and when these were held to the light they showed what looked like pastel flowers or designs. (Berlitz and Moore, 1980: 72 and 96)

Although these descriptions sound very much like what you might expect to find in the wreckage of a downed balloon and its related cargo and nothing at all like what you might expect to find at the site of a flying saucer crash, they are taken to be proof of the extraterrestrial nature of the crashed object.

Furthermore, Berlitz and Moore attach to the Roswell account a certain description of the Roswell aliens supposedly recovered from the wreckage. This would depart from the common description of crashed extraterrestrials as simply diminutive humans and instead incorporate details that have more in common with those popularized in the film *Close Encounters of the Third Kind*. Details derived from 'several medical informants' are cited as the source of their claims.

Approximate height between three and a half and four and a half feet tall.

The head, by human standards, is oversize in relation to torso and limbs. Although brain capacity has not been specified it is considerably larger comparatively than that possessed by human beings.

Head and body are hairless though some report a slight fuzz on pate.

Eyes are large and deep-set or sunken, far apart, and slightly slanted.

No ear lobes or extending flesh beyond apertures noted on each side of the head.

Nose is formless, with nares indicated by only a slight protuberance.

Mouth is a small slit which may not function as an orifice for food ingestion. No mention of teeth. . . .

Neck is relatively thin.

Arms and legs are extremely thin, with arms reaching nearly to knee sections.

Hands show four fingers and no thumb, with two fingers double the length of the others. Fingernails are elongated. A slight webbing effect exists between the fingers.

UFO religion

> Skin of tough texture and grayish. Skin on some preserved bodies appeared dark brown, evidently charred.
>
> Blood is liquid but not similar to human blood by color or any known blood type.
>
> There were conflicting reports on reproductive organs, with some observers reporting no distinguishing sex characteristics while others stated that there were distinctive male and female bodies sexually comparable to human beings. (Berlitz and Moore, 1980: 110–12)

With these details the Roswell crash story was pretty much complete, though proponents of the truth of the event would continually squabble over the details. The heart of the story was the same as the Aurora and Aztec stories. A flying saucer crashed in the American Southwest. Remains of the craft were distinguished by indecipherable hieroglyphic-type writing. The crew of the craft, clearly extraterrestrial in origin, were found dead at the scene.

◆ ◆ ◆

A few years ago I convinced my wife and a couple of our best friends to take our summer vacation in Roswell, New Mexico. Don't ask me how I convinced them. Let's just say I can be very persuasive when I have to be. We were in Roswell during what must have been the off season. I say this because the streets of downtown Roswell were nothing like the descriptions I had read of the July 4, 1997 celebration of the fiftieth anniversary of the crash. The streets were vacant. There were a few saucer-related businesses, most of which sold cheap UFO novelties and tee shirts. The UFO Museum and Research Center was open, but more than a little dull. There was a replica of the Roswell saucer crash site, a replica of a scene right out of the alien autopsy film, paintings and other artistic interpretations of the scene, and a gift shop selling the same merchandise that could be found across the street. When I asked about the crash site it was clear that the woman at the counter wasn't really interested in helping me. I was told that the drive out was long and boring, that the climate was far too hot for us to have any enjoyment, and that there wasn't anything to see except sand and brush. Overall, it was something of a disappointment, except for the alien streetlights up and down the block. The Roswell crash seemed almost to have played out, as if the crash debris and the crash story were already being swept away and forgotten, like Aurora, Aztec, and Roswell itself in an earlier time, not by the military or intelligence agents but by the movement of popular culture, which is never content to let passing fads do anything but pass.

Such passing is a constant threat to nuts and bolts ufology because if you don't come up with a few examples of said nuts and bolts sooner or later, people will begin to have doubts. This is more true of saucer crashes than of those ineffable UFO sightings. As long as the nuts and bolts are up in the sky no one has any reason to expect tangible physical evidence, but once they make it to the ground, especially once they crash and spread debris all around, someone had better come up with something, even if it is just a few nuts and bolts. Of course, despite many claims to the contrary, that is precisely what those who are Roswell believers have failed to do.

I picked up a piece of debris evidence at the Roswell Museum and Research Center, an I-beam based on the description of the crash debris given by Jesse Marcel Jr., son of the Jesse Marcel who originally gathered the materials for the Roswell base. According to the literature that accompanied my I-beam replica:

> This I-Beam replica was developed to recreate what Jesse A. Marcel Jr., M.D. remembers seeing in Roswell, New Mexico, as an 11 year old in 1947. Dr. Marcel Jr. actually had the opportunity to hold the original I-Beam and other pieces of the debris in his hand. Dr. Marcel, Jr. clearly recalls that the I-Beam resembled aluminum and that unusual violet symbols lined one side of the slim piece. . . . The I-Beam replica is a visual reproduction only. It is not intended to replicate the strength and other characteristics of the original I-Beam. Its strange symbols are based on a description of ten specific shapes described by Dr. Marcel, Jr. Their violet color was identified by Dr. Marcel, Jr. as 'PMS 264' which is an exact shade according to the Pantone color matching system used by artists and printers.

And then, at the end, as if to make one final argument for the authenticity of the piece:

> One of the four original aluminum I-Beam Replicas and other crash debris replicas are on permanent display at the

UFO religion

International UFO Museum and Research Center in Roswell, New Mexico.

Did you catch that? If one reads it quickly it almost sounds as if an example of an actual I-beam from the crashed saucer is on display at the museum, as if what you hold in your hands is a plastic replica of the real thing, the real nuts and bolts of a flying saucer. But, of course, that is not what is said at all. The only thing on display at the museum is an aluminum replica, no closer to the real thing than the twenty-dollar piece of plastic you now hold in your hands. If the plastic I-beam is a replica of the aluminum I-beam, what is the aluminum I-beam a replica of?

Keyhoe, Edwards and Hynek turned the mysterious into a mystery to be solved with facts and figures. Roswell 1997 turned a moment of real uncertainty and wonder for the world of 1947 into something more shamelessly commercial than anything that could have been dreamed up by Dr. Gee at Aztec. Roswell 1997 transformed our alien visitors into plastic dioramas, not with a powerful beam built by our brightest scientists but by the same commercial industry that brought us Space Mountain. The fear of the unknown can't be called forth at a theme park, however, where the dinosaurs don't bite and the guns don't kill. Wonder in the face of infinity is beyond the powers of Disney magic to induce. Street carnivals in desert towns; television specials; and plastic replicas of flying saucers, extraterrestrial entities, and crash debris that aren't really replicas of anything, only make it all seem cheap and silly.

What is the aluminum I-beam a replica of? It is a replica of nothing. It is either nothing more than yet another attempt to make money out of other people's fears and fantasies or, as I like to believe, nothing less than an attempt to substantiate the long ago childhood memories of a boy who faced the unknown, held the remnants of a flying saucer, and felt the chill of fear as if the relic in his hand had been nothing less than a splinter from the cross of Jesus; as if the tin foil spread out by his dad on the kitchen table was a sign that the end was near; as if the Russians, or the Martians, were closer than anyone ever dreamed; all of that accompanied by a sense of wonder, a sense of expectation, a sense of adventure. I know that feeling and I know that it can't be captured in plastic any more than it can be cataloged and classified. I know that feeling. It all started with a crash in Aurora; the ships themselves, swore Dr. Gee, were fueled by the same magnetic power that generates the aurora borealis; our own anxieties fueled by northern lights, strange fragments of the space age, flying saucers, and cold war fears. It all started with our own hopes fueled by lights in the sky, by one small step for man, by dreams of a future different from the past.

3

Conspiracies

The forbidding landscape around Groom Lake, Nevada has to be one of the loneliest spots on planet earth. Having just left the very terrestrial, very human, very American city of Las Vegas, the contrast is striking. This is an alien landscape, sand and death stretching for miles in every direction. I can almost believe that I am an explorer on some strange planet, all alone in an unknown world. Even the Joshua trees that dot the landscape seem unearthly. One might almost believe that they themselves are the bizarre inhabitants of some Martian valley, moving too slowly to be noticed by human observers, but nevertheless moving under the direction of their own alien intelligence, their own non-human will. Then I notice something that proves that I am still on the earth but offers me little comfort. On the Joshua trees are perched ravens, big and black, sitting still and dark as if they have grown there, the strange fruit of a supernatural orchard. Now this feels less like Mars and more like Hell, more like a dream best forgotten. After that, it only gets worse. Out here, in the middle of nowhere, in as god-forsaken a place as you will find, the terrain is suddenly broken by a line of red posts forming a fence without rails. Ahead are the signs that I have been looking for, the ones I had hoped were not real. They are real. They flank both sides of the roadway at the bottom of a small canyon. There is no way to miss them.

RESTRICTED AREA
NO TRESPASSING

And then, in small red letters, the bit that I had hoped was only a legend.

Use of deadly force authorized.

To my left, half-way up the hillside, I spot some sort of electronic sensor, mounted on a tripod and looking for all the world like an alien probe. To my right, I see the same. Am I back on Mars again? Then a flash from the hillside to my right attracts my attention. Now I know that I am not on Mars, now I know that this is not a dream. The flash is from the door of a truck. Two men have climbed out and are watching me, one of them with binoculars. I have the feeling that if I was to attempt to cross the red fence line I might find myself in a lot of trouble. So this is Area 51?

— Area 51 —

In the 1950s Nevada's Groom Lake, a dry lakebed in a very isolated region north of Las Vegas, became an important site for the development and testing of American military aircraft. Chosen because of its isolation as well as the geographical features of the site, Groom Lake was one of the US government's most secret installations. The U-2 spy plane, designed to fly over the USSR on reconnaissance missions in an effort to determine the strength of the Soviet military, was housed at Groom Lake. Later, the site would be used in the development of other, equally secretive, military aircraft. Its existence, and the government's denial of the same, have long been a source of speculation and controversy. It was in the late 1980s, however, that Groom Lake, or Area 51 as it is better known, came to be clearly associated with flying saucers.

It was in 1989 that Bob Lazar announced that he was breaking his oath of secrecy concerning his employment at Area 51. The story he told was far more provocative than a story of spy planes or top-secret government activities. It was a story of flying saucers and alien technology. According to his story, Lazar went to work at Area 51 in 1988. There he was required to sign a secrecy oath as well as a waiver of his constitutional rights, an illegal requirement that was

3. The long road to Area 51 near Rachel, Nevada

authorized by a document signed by Ronald Reagan. It was not long after his arrival on the base that Lazar came to realize the shocking nature of the work he was to perform. Within minutes of arriving on the base Lazar was led through a hangar and shown a shiny metallic disc some thirty-five feet in diameter. He was then provided with a folder of classified information even more startling than the disc itself. According to David Darlington in his excellent book *Area 51: The Dreamland Chronicles*:

> In the first folder Bob found, to his unfolding astonishment, eight-by-ten glossy photographs of nine flying saucers. One looked like the object in the hangar ... the others differed in shape from one to the next. There were also photos from an alleged autopsy that had been performed on one of the craft's original operators, sarcastically called 'the Kids.' Lazar would later describe the figure as a 'typical' gray alien: short and hair-

less with a large head, small nose and mouth, and big, dark, almond-shaped eyes. A single organ, apparently capable of performing several bodily functions, was exposed with the carcass. (Darlington, 1997: 70)

Lazar would later learn that the Kids were visitors from the Zeta Reticuli star system, specifically from the fourth planet of the second sun in the binary system.

Several research projects were underway in regards to the extraterrestrials and their craft. First, Project Sidekick involved research into a beam weapon found on the spacecraft. Second, Project Looking Glass was investigating the possibility of looking backward in time. Finally, Project Galileo was concerned with the saucers' propulsion system and, specifically, their ability to travel great distances in what must have been a relatively short period of time. It was to this project that Lazar was assigned. The Kids had purportedly helped in these projects until 1979, when a soldier's refusal to heed a warning from one of the ETs resulted in the death of a number of humans.

Lazar's friend Gene Huff describes the work on Project Galileo in this way:

Bob had been hired to be part of a 'back engineering' team. Back engineering is the act of taking apart a finished product to find out what makes it tick. In this instance, their job was to back engineer a flying disc to see if it could be reproduced with earth materials. Bob's specific job was to help back engineer the propulsion system. In subsequent trips to S4 Bob was exposed to the propulsion system on a bench in a lab, as well as the propulsion system, in place, in a disc. In a sleek disc he would eventually nickname the 'sport model' Bob had to hang upside down through an opening on the floor of the central level to view the gravity amplifiers on the lower level. He eventually witnessed a brief, low altitude test flight of this same disc. He was also taught how the discs are able to distort space/time to achieve interstellar travel. The 'Sport Model' disc is currently being produced as a plastic model by the Testor Corporation. (As posted to alt.conspiracy.area51 newsgroup, March 12, 1995)

According to Lazar's story, he risked his job and his freedom to show what he had learned to his friends. Knowing the time and date of saucer test flights, Lazar arranged to accompany his friends to a spot outside the base where he knew the craft could be seen in flight. Gene Huff describes his experiences in the company of Lazar:

> The disc . . . staged a breathtaking performance. . . . At first it seemed far away, then you'd blink and it would seem a lot closer, then you'd blink again and it would seem a LOT closer. It wasn't the same sensation as seeing a set of headlights on a car or landing lights on a jet approach you at night time. There was no sense of continual movement toward you, it just sort of 'jumps' toward you and this is very alarming to your brain. Bob explained that this is because of its method of propulsion and the way it distorts space/time and light. Bob also explained that the bright glow of the disc was due to the way it was energized. When the disc came our direction, it glowed so brightly that we thought it might explode so we moved behind the open trunk lid for protection. The fact is that an explosion was the only thing, other than the sun, that we had ever seen that bright so that's why we suspected an explosion. As we all look back on that now, it's difficult to believe it came so close that we backed away from it. After all, it was probably still a few miles away and that fact reflects how brightly it was glowing. But the fact is, it did come that close and the event was much more thrilling than I've described here. It, too, eventually sat down behind the mountains and we left. (As posted to alt.conspiracy.area51 newsgroup, March 12, 1995)

Even more provocative than the technological revelations associated with the recovered saucers was the historical and philosophical information that had been learned from the Kids and shared with Lazar. Lazar claims that he was given documents that told the history of 'Sol Three,' or the earth, from the point of view of the visitors from Reticulum Four. These documents revealed that extraterrestrials had completed dozens of genetic manipulations on human beings throughout history. In addition, earth's spiritual leaders, including Jesus, had been created directly by alien scientists to shape the course of human development.

Lazar's story was presented to the world in the form of a television program hosted by Las Vegas TV personality George Knapp. The story gathered an incredible amount of media attention and before long UFO seekers from all over the world were traveling to Groom Lake in the hope of getting a view of a flying saucer. The influx of people and the amount of media interest in Area 51 prompted the government to expand the base boundaries in an attempt to keep civilians even farther away. This action, of course, only strengthened the belief among the public that something strange was going on at Groom Lake.

The nearby town of Rachel, Nevada was quick to seize upon the Area 51/Flying Saucer craze. The town, not really much more than a trailer park in the middle of the dessert, had only two businesses, a gas station and the Rachel Bar and Grill. The Bar and Grill changed its name to the Little A'Le'Inn, added a few rooms to accommodate some of the many visitors to Area 51, and soon became the central meeting place for all those interested in spying on the government's operations. Rachel, Nevada was suddenly the center of conspiracy-minded ufological investigations. Throughout the area every small business was suddenly selling itself and its merchandise with the help of alien iconography.

When I finally visited Rachel, Nevada in the spring of 2006, evidence of its early 1990s boom was still evident, as was the fact that the boom had long ago run its course. Bob Lazar had been arrested for involvement in an illegal Las Vegas brothel and the level of his exposure to the activities of Groom Lake had been called into

4. Highway 375 near Area 51 in Nevada

5. A billboard near Area 51

question. Rachel was still set up to appeal to the few saucer seekers who dared to brave the desert, however. One billboard outside town advertised 'Alien Fresh Jerky,' whatever that is. The road running by Groom Lake and Rachel was marked by official signage from the State of Nevada naming it 'The Extraterrestrial Highway.' In Rachel proper, an old and weathered plywood sign showed an alien leaping over a candlestick – an ad for a gift-and-candle shop. The local gas station had a sign depicting flying saucers with the word 'Gas' written in big red letters high atop a utility pole. An old wrecker truck hoisting a crashed saucer in the air was parked out front of the Little A'Le'Inn, weaving together the Roswell crash story and the Area 51 mythology in one iconic image. Inside the establishment I found pretty much what I expected, friendly bar service, tables for enjoying the restaurant's short orders, and lots and lots of UFO collectibles, most of which seemed almost identical to the souvenirs for sale at Roswell.

On my way out of town and back towards Las Vegas I kept straining my eyes to see one of the mysterious craft written about by Lazar. The road signs along the way warned of 'Low Flying Aircraft' but I saw neither terrestrial nor extraterrestrial craft flying either low or high. I did catch a glimpse of something odd in the sky on a couple of occasions, but upon closer inspection they turned out to be plastic shopping bags carried aloft by the desert winds. Area 51 had revealed no flying saucers. Groom Lake had kept her secrets, secrets I am sure she has. Over the mountains from Rachel, through the warning signs, between the red posts, past the electronic surveillance equipment, and beyond the sentries, there are secrets. Area 51 may not house sport model flying saucers and extraterrestrials known as the Kids, but I am sure that it holds secrets and conspiracies and I am sure that lethal force is authorized to keep them.

— Reverse Engineering —

In *The Day after Roswell* (1997), Col. Philip J. Corso (Ret.) added yet another conspiratorial element to the crashed saucer/government cover-up mythos. In a story that blends together elements of Frank Scully's Dr. Gee, the Roswell crash story, and Lazar's account of Area 51, Corso relates his experiences as part of a military team responsible for reverse engineering the Roswell crash saucer debris. His charge was to analyze the Roswell crash debris and then to place the alien technology in the hands of private industry for research and development. The debris consisted of six basic elements and, as described by Corso, is clearly reminiscent of earlier descriptions, with some important additions.

1) [T]iny, clear, single filament, flexible glasslike wires twisted together through a kind of gray harness as if they were cable going into a junction. . . .

2) [T]hin two-inch-around matte gray oyster cracker-shaped wafers of a material that looked like plastic but had tiny road maps of wires barely raised/etched along the surface. . . .

3) [A] two-piece set of dark elliptical eyepieces as thin as skin. The Walter Reed pathologists said they adhered to the lenses of the extraterrestrial creatures' eyes and seemed to reflect existing light, even in what looked like complete darkness. . . .

4) There was a dull, grayish-silvery foil-like swatch of cloth among those artifacts that you could not fold, bend, tear, or wad up but that bounded right back into its original shape without any creases. It was a metallic fiber with physical characteristics that would later be called 'supertenacity.' . . .

5) [A] short, stubby flashlight almost with a self-contained power source that was nothing at all like a battery. The scientists at Wright Field who examined it said they couldn't see the beam of light shoot out of it, but when they pointed the pencil-like flashlight at a wall, they could see a tiny circle of red light, but there was no actual beam from the end of what seemed like a lens to the wall. . . .

6) [T]he strangest device of all, a headband, almost, with electrical-signal pickup devices on either side. I could figure out no use for this thing whatever unless whoever used it did so as a fancy hair band. (Corso, 1997: 47–50)

Considering the descriptions of these materials and the nature of Corso's central claim, it comes as no surprise when Corso reports that the reverse engineering of these items resulted in the development of some of the most important technological advances of the last decades. The glasslike wires resulted in the development of what we know today as fiber optics. The oyster cracker shaped wafers led to the development of the integrated circuit chip. The eyepieces are responsible for night vision technology. The foil-like cloth has been transformed into supertenacity fiber technology. Finally, the short, stubby flashlight represents the origin of the laser.

Corso agrees with many Roswell researchers that the 1947 saucer crash was followed by a major government cover-up. This cover-up was not just about protecting society from the truth of extraterrestrial visitors, however, but was also about keeping knowledge of that recovery from falling into the hands of America's enemies. While one of these enemies was clearly the Soviet Union, Corso argues that a far greater enemy was extraterrestrial in origin. As a matter of fact, much of the cold war with the Soviets served as cover for a far more frightening conflict with the aliens. The Strategic Defense Initiative, also known as President Reagan's 'Star Wars' program, was thus meant as a deterrent for a war that would be fought on two fronts. As the government stated publicly, it was meant to protect the US from Soviet missiles, but it was also meant to protect the US from alien invasion. The 'Star Wars' program, implementing much of the technology that had been reverse engineered from Roswell, was an attempt to use alien technology to protect America from the aliens themselves. Indeed, Corso sounds quite self-congratulatory when he claims that the US is now very well protected against the threat of alien invasion, in large part because of the work he and his team did in facilitating the analysis and development of the Roswell wreckage.

He writes:

> I understand that we were fighting a Cold War with the Soviets and a skirmish war with extraterrestrials. I believed that their intentions were, and still are, hostile, and I believe that we took the steps necessary to develop the weapons that can blunt their threat. In fact, the US military has better, more accurate, and more powerful weapons for killing UFOs than were deployed in the movie *Independence Day*.

Likewise:

> We can knock these guys down tomorrow with high-energy lasers and directed Particle beam weapons that come right out of a *Star Wars* movie. And these aren't fiction, they're fact. If you want to know more, pay a visit to the US Army Space Command Website on the Internet. These missile-launched HELs are the pride of our planetary defense system and a direct result of President Reagan's courage in pushing for the Strategic Defense Initiative when everyone said it wouldn't work. And that SDI was a direct result of the work General Troudeau and I did at Army R&D in 1962. (Corso, 1997: 299)

Not only did Ronald Reagan bring the Soviet Union to its knees and the Berlin Wall crashing to the ground, but he also protected the earth from an imminent invasion from extraterrestrial enemies. The secrets of Area 51, therefore, are surely secrets justified by the circumstances. If the alien technology had fallen into the hands of the Soviets they would have used the technology against us. In addition, they would have tried to forge an alliance with the extraterrestrials. By maintaining the secret of Roswell the US government was able to both defeat the Soviets and keep the aliens at bay. Sleep well, Corso seems to say, the secret conspiracy works in your favor. Area 51 should not be frightening, but comforting. Trust us (the American government/military establishment), for we have done a good job of protecting you from threats most of you don't even believe are real. If we have to keep a few things secret and threaten to use deadly force against our own citizens, or if we have to place millions of dollars in black budget programs with little or no accountability to the citizenry, it is for the best. Whether one believes in flying saucers and Roswell wreckage or not, Corso's claim is the same: be comforted, not frightened, by secret bases in the desert.

Having seen that red fence line, having had my presence noted by high-tech equipment, having been watched through binoculars by unidentified individuals, and having read that sign – *the use of deadly force is authorized* – I confess that I understand why many people remain a little frightened. Corso's assurances just aren't enough to put all those worried minds at ease. Corso sees the government as the white knight coming to the rescue of a world unaware of the threats that it faces, but his version of reality is in sharp contrast to that held by those who have answered a knock on their door to be greeted by the Men in Black.

— Men in Black —

In 1957 Gray Barker, who had broken into the flying saucer field with his book recording the story of the Flatwoods, West Virginia monster sightings, published a book that would introduce the Men in Black to the UFO community. While Jim Keith in *Casebook on the Men in Black* (1997) makes a good case that strange figures dressed in black play a part in much ancient mythology it was in Gray Barker's *They Knew Too Much about Flying Saucers* (1997, first published 1956) that the idea of mysterious characters attired in black came to be associated with the flying saucer mystery. In this book Barker tells the story of Albert K. Bender, founder and president of the International Flying Saucer Bureau (IFSB), who in 1953 announced that the flying saucer mystery had been solved and subsequently discontinued his involvement in all things saucerian. Barker's quest was to discover what Bender had learned, why he could not talk about it, and to whom he was answering. All Barker knew for sure was that Bender had been contacted by three men dressed in black.

> I do not wish to get Bender into trouble. I don't believe publishing this information will endanger him. If I did, I'd keep my mouth shut.
>
> I believe Bender handled himself too well for trouble. Some of the information he gave us may have been intended to lead us away from an actual solution. If that was the case I can heartily appreciate his position.
>
> If Bender was closed down by the United States government, the three men probably had good reasons. But Bender never told us who the three men were, or who sent them, only that they 'showed credentials.' But government men do not dress so conspicuously, especially if they are on a secret mission.
>
> All the three men were dressed similarly – in black. (Barker, 1997: 94–5)

According to Barker the 'Bender Mystery' began when Bender published two special announcements in *Space Review*, the official publication of the IFSB. The Men in Black had told Bender what to write and had then edited the copy. First, Bender wrote:

> LATE BULLETIN: A source, which the IFSB considers very reliable, has informed us that the investigation of the flying saucer mystery and the solution is approaching its final stages.
>
> This same source to whom we had preferred data, which had come into our possession, suggested that it was not the proper method and time to publish this data in *Space Review*.

This was followed by a second announcement:

> STATEMENT OF IMPORTANCE: The mystery of the flying saucers is no longer a mystery. The source is already known, but any information about this is being withheld by orders from a higher source. We would like to print the full story in *Space Review* but because of the nature of the information we are very sorry that we have been advised in the negative.
>
> We advise those engaged in saucer work to please be very cautious. (Bender, 1968: 110 and 111)

Of course, what are left out of Bender's announcements are the very facts that Barker believes crucial. They reveal nothing about the supposed answer to the 'mystery of the flying saucers' or about the nature of the 'higher source' to which Bender seemed to answer. Barker writes:

> There may be such things as flying saucers from space, and these things from space may have people or things in them that mean to do us harm.
>
> We can fight these things off, somehow, with bullets, or prayers, or some new invention that we are bound to come up with if we have to. I am not alarmed about bug-eyed monsters, little green men, or dero [more on these later!] who may or may not be shooting at us with rays from far underground.
>
> Something else disturbs me far more.
>
> There exists forces or agencies which would prevent us from finding out whether or not there are such green men, or bug-eyed monsters, or saucers with things in them.
>
> I have a feeling that some day there will come a slow knocking at my door.
>
> They will be at your door, too, unless we all get wise and find out who the three men really are. (Barker, 1997: 246)

The answer to the Bender Mystery would not be revealed until 1962, when Barker was able to persuade Bender to tell the full story in *Flying Saucers and the Three Men*. In Bender's account we learn that his encounter with the three men began after he had organized the International Flying Saucer Bureau to attempt psychic contact with the alien intelligences behind the flying saucers. Following this experiment he was contacted by the three men in black.

> Their clothing was made of a black material which reminded me of cloth used in the attire of clergymen. It was well pressed, appeared almost new. All the other apparel, such as ties, shirt, stockings, and shoes was also black. They wore hats, of Homburg style, also black. Their faces were unpleasant to look at. Their eyes shone like tiny flashlight bulbs, and the teeth were pearly white, set in a very dark complexion. I could not see their hands, covered by black gloves. A bluish radiance enveloped their entire bodies, and I wondered if this was giving off the sulphuric odor.

Their words matched their mysterious appearance; they told Bender,

> You will see all three of us again, but we shall not reveal our names, as they would mean nothing to you. Refer to us as 'Num-

bers 1, 2, and 3.' We will answer according to number. (Bender, 1968: 87 and 75)

Bender reported that the Men in Black had transported him to their spacecraft. His account marks what may be considered one of the first of the abduction narratives that would become so important in the following decades.

> The darkness cleared away and I was suddenly surrounded by a brilliant glow, as if the beam of a large searchlight had suddenly hit me in the eyes. As my eyes grew accustomed to the brilliance, I began to make out my surroundings. I was in a huge, circular room with a glass dome. The walls gave me the impression of stainless steel, but they seemed to give off light, accounting for their unusual glitter.

Furthermore,

> Two of them remained beside me as the other walked into the shadows and returned with a metal vial containing a liquid which they poured over my body. Then the three massaged the liquid into my skin. As they did so my body became warm as if heat had been applied. They massaged every part of my body without exception, turning me over on my stomach and my sides. . . . When I was completely anointed they left the room, and a large round object was lowered from the ceiling until it was four or five feet above my body. It gradually began to glow, giving off a lavender light, until it changed to a deep purple hue. (Bender, 1968: 78 and 129)

Bender learned that the extraterrestrials operated a secret base in Antarctica, that they were on earth to extract vital elements from terrestrial water, and that they often kidnapped earth people in order to take possession of their bodies, which they would then inhabit and use to move around unrecognized. He was taken to Antarctica and allowed to witness part of the water treatment process. He was also allowed a short glimpse of the aliens in their true form, hideous creatures resembling the Flatwoods Monster described earlier by Gray Barker!

The extraterrestrials provided Bender with a great deal of information. They informed him that there was water on the moon, that their species lived on mushrooms, and that there are races that live within the hollow interior of the planet earth who are responsible for the ghostly apparitions sometimes witnessed by surface folk. They also assured him that there was no god. Bender reported that he was now free to tell the truth about the flying saucers because the extraterrestrials had completed their mission and left the earth. Thus, Bender was no longer bound to silence.

The fact that Bender reported that the Men in Black had completed their mission and left the earth did not, of course, mean that the presence of the Men in Black would no longer be a part of saucerian speculations – far from it. The presence of Men in Black in UFO accounts has continued unabated despite Bender's assurance that they had taken what they wanted and gone away. By the 1990s they even starred in their own series of Hollywood movies, an animated Saturday morning children's program, and a ride at Universal Studios Theme Park. Barker and Bender have been long forgotten by popular culture. The Men in Black live on.

Jim Keith has cataloged encounters with the Men in Black (MIB) dating from the Middle Ages to the present day and has concluded that stories involving these mysterious figures have many possible explanations. For example, Keith claims that at least a part of all MIB sightings are related to secret governmental activities. Keith suggests that government agents often appear to UFO witnesses in the guise of the Men in Black in order to scare them into retracting or limiting their testimony. The Roswell saucer crash offers a clear example of this as some of the witnesses have reported that their families were warned by agents in dark attire that they must tell no one of what they had seen. Keith writes:

> The US government has been involved in monitoring and harassing witnesses of UFO phenomena since the earliest days of its public notoriety, in the late 1940's. Part of their activities may involve copycatting the weirder MIB encounters by wearing black suits, driving black cars, and perhaps engaging in other weird harassment techniques, including delivering electronic sounds over the telephone. The purpose of this, quite simply, is to scare the wits out of UFO observers and contactees, but also in some instances to confuse the origin of high-tech aerial craft tested, particularly, in the US. (Keith, 1997: 218)

In addition to government agents, however, Keith also suggests that some encounters with the MIB are actually encounters with members of secret occult organizations, such as the Black Lodge. He notes that many UFO contactees have themselves been very interested in occult activities. In addition, some MIB encounters are the products of delusions, showing only that the experiencer has been influenced by movies, cartoons, books, and other elements of mass culture.

And, of course, Keith admits that some encounters are surely the result of hoaxes, with the Barker/Bender story being a possible example. It has been suggested that Barker may have sent three men dressed all in black to Bender's apartment as a joke. When Bender seemed to take the visitation seriously, Barker developed the Bender Mystery as a way to take the joke to the next level. Even Bender's own book is thought by some to have been ghost written by Barker as a way to elaborate on the story that he himself had instigated. For Barker, the hoax just got bigger and bigger.

Finally, Keith insists that some of the encounters with the Men have been actual encounters with what he calls 'Supernatural Men in Black.' As a matter of fact, all of the other explanations for the MIB are parasitic upon the experiences with real-life supernatural and unearthly forces. Whether or not Keith sees these supernatural entities as visitors from another planet or another dimension, as beings from outer space or demonic forces, is unclear. Perhaps he means to leave the final answer ambiguous. Nevertheless, ambiguous though they may be, they are, according to Keith, very real.

> Finally, there seems to be an actual MIB experience that is unexplainable in terms of strict materialism, or known data: that cannot be reduced to materialistic causation. These Men in Black manifest in seamless progression throughout the ages, unchanged for the most part except for the definitions that we apply to them. In ancient times they were fairies and trolls and demons, now they are the 'UFO silencers.' (Keith, 1997: 220)

Something tells me that Gray Barker would not be worried by any of this, whether the Men in Black come from outer space, Washington, DC or hell itself. In the epilogue of Bender's book, Barker wrote:

Now that Bender has cleared up so many mysteries surrounding his closing and erased many of my original fears, it is necessary that I come up with some additional bogiemen, for I am by natural composition a coward who enjoys being afraid of the dark. I have conjured up many such bogiemen since reading Bender's manuscript, but I have space in which to warn you only of one tremendous fear.

The editor of a popular saucer publication, in criticizing my book, claimed he had found out who the three men actually were and identified them by name: 'Boredom, Frustration, and Disgust.' These three men, unfortunately, are often real, and lurk constantly in the shadows. You may be their next victim. These three men, as abstract and tenuous as they may seem, work desperately to perform their terrible tasks;

They attempt to silence you and prevent your telling what you already may know about flying saucers. They attempt to divert your mind to more 'normal' interests so that you cannot carry out your research. They cannot be killed by bullets. They will not just go away because you may ignore them or not believe in them.

They can be defeated only with imagination, courage, good humor, and good will. (Bender, 1968: 160)

Imagination, courage, good humor, and good will . . . I think Barker just might have the right idea about this UFO thing. Though perhaps he should have added 'good taste' to his list . . .

— Cattle Mutilation —

In 1989 the town of Fyffe, Alabama, a small village located at the southern tip of the Appalachian Mountain range, was suddenly thrust into the UFO spotlight. In February of that year a local resident reported a sighting of an unidentified flying object. Within just a few weeks of the initial sighting the Associated Press was reporting that more than four thousand visitors had journeyed to Fyffe in the interest of spotting a saucer for themselves. This more than doubled the town's population. The sighting of a UFO would soon seem unimpressive to the town's residents, however, as they uncovered evidence that many believed pointed to an alien agenda that included the killing and mutilation of livestock.

Though unconfirmed, the Fyffe Police Department is reported to have issued a press release signed by Charles 'Junior' Garmany, chief of police; Boyd Graben, mayor; and Ted Oliphant, investigating officer (http://www.mufor.org/fyffe.htm). The press release indicated that the Fyffe Police Department had been conducting an investigation of cattle mutilations in cooperation with other law enforcement agencies. Beginning on October 20, 1992, it was reported that at the time of the press release more than one hundred animals had been found dead and mutilated, with 'various internal organs missing.' They wrote:

> The incisions examined on the animals exhibit a precise surgical cutting. In many of the cases there has been evidence of extremely high heat at the tissue excisions. The absence of physical evidence adds to the mystery at the majority of mutilation sites. Though many animals have been found in soft pasture land, and in many cases mud, there have been no footprints, tracks, or marks found anywhere near the mutilated animals.

Despite the number of cases no one had managed to establish either a suspect or a motive in the cases.

The first mutilation in the Fyffe area was reported to have happened on the farm of John Strawn. One of Strawn's cattle was discovered by a neighbor: 'The animal's entire milk sac was missing with no evidence of blood on the animal, nor on the ground where it lay. The neighbor said the neat, oval incision where the udder had been removed appeared to be charred.' Soon, other area farmers were reporting similar incidents of dead cattle marked by surgical incisions and the removal of organs.

> In many cases the rectum had been cored out neatly, with no evidence of blood or body fluid present. On female livestock the sex organs had been removed in an identical fashion with clean, bloodless incisions. On male livestock, the sex organs had also been removed, again in oval, bloodless incisions.

In addition to the physical details associated with the carcasses, it was also reported that helicopters were seen or heard in an area around the time that the animal was found. One case was particularly strange because of the physical evidence discovered on the scene.

> On January 31, 1993, a rancher in the Dawson Community led investigators to the carcass of a Black Angus cow. The animal's

genitals and rectum had been cored out in one large incision that left a hole the size of coffee can. The animal's jaw had been completely stripped in an oval incision that encompassed the entire right side of the animal's face. The tongue was completely gone, cut deep down into the throat. There was no blood present on the animal itself, nor on the ground surrounding it.

Further examination revealed a flaky white material on the animal's right rib cage and on the ground five (5) feet from the carcass. The material was placed in the empty wrapper of a cigarette pack and transported to the Fyffe Police Department where it was transferred to a glass jar. While removing the flaky particles from the cigarette wrapper, the material came in contact with the brass tip of a ball-point pen. Within one second of contact with the brass, the material melted into an almost clear liquid. To reduce the risk of this happening to the remaining material, the rest was shaken out into a jar where it remained unaffected. This white, flaky material was then air expressed to a molecular biologist at a leading eastern University for analysis.

According to the press release, it was determined that the substance was composed of aluminum, titanium, oxygen and silicon. It was also found to contain titanium in an amount that, according to the scientist, was larger 'than he would ever expect to see in any substance and that there was no way this combination of elements could ever occur in nature.' The press release concluded with an appeal to the different branches of government to find a quick solution to the mystery.

> Police Chief Junior Garmany and Mayor Boyd Graben, themselves involved in farming, believe the results of our investigation require further attention. It is incumbent on all of us Military, state and federal government to assist farmers to find out who the phantom surgeons are. It seems basic to help the man who is responsible for ensuring there is food available for our dinner tables. The farmer is not interested in politically correct official explanations. He wants to know what has happened to his livestock. It should be the responsibility of all law-enforcement to join together to find an answer to this problem that is adversely affecting the cattle farmer, here in Alabama.

What remained unsaid in the press release was the theory that was on everyone's mind and all over the news reports, the theory that the mutilations were performed by extraterrestrials for reasons that appear incomprehensible, and that the federal government, its presence revealed by the helicopters, was for some reason complicit in the activities.

The idea that extraterrestrials might be responsible for the surgical incisions and organ removals that accompanied the cattle deaths did not originate in Fyffe, Alabama. In the early 1970s reports of cattle mutilations were common in many parts of the American Midwest and Canada. Brought to popular attention by the journalist Linda Mouton Howe, these 'mutilations' were generally distinguished by several features.

First, the cows are found dead with the cause of death undetermined. Second, all blood is found to have been removed from the cow without any sign of blood on the surrounding ground. Third, several of the cow's organs, including their reproductive organs, seem to have been surgically removed. Fourth, the carcasses often exhibit high radiation levels and repel the sorts of scavengers one might expect them to attract. Fifth, there is no evidence of footprints at the site of the killing. Sixth, marks and abrasions are often found on the animal's legs, indicating that it may have been moved from the location and then returned. Finally, such mutilations are often accompanied by sightings of unidentified flying objects and black helicopters.

According to Howe and others, there are several possible explanations for the facts so described. The killings and mutilations could have been completed as part of the religious activities of a satanic cult. The killings and mutilations might also be the result of some secret government experiment. Third, there may be nothing strange about these deaths and the concerns expressed by those involved may be simply a form of mass hysteria. Finally, and usually the most well received of the theories, the mutilations may be the result of some strange extraterrestrial activities, carried out with the knowledge of the federal government.

Most scientific researchers, including those acting on behalf of the FBI, have concluded that the cattle deaths are the result of natural causes and that the 'mutilations' are nothing more than the work of insects and other small scavengers that typically devour soft tissue on the outside of the body before larger scavengers begin their work, or that clean up the rough edges left by larger scavengers resulting in what appear to be 'surgical incisions.' Likewise, such insects tend to clean up any blood or tissue that is on the ground much more quickly than one might think.

Of course this doesn't explain the black helicopters or the UFO sightings. Nor does it address the eyewitness account of cattle abduction reported in the *Yates Center (Kansas) Farmer's Advocate* of April 23, 1897. Yes, 1897. Once again twentieth-century saucerian lore has its roots in the great airship mystery of a century past. The following is the account of Alexander Hamilton, local farmer.

> Last Monday night about 10:30 we were awakened by a noise among the cattle. I arose thinking that perhaps my bulldog was performing pranks, but upon going to the door saw to my utter astonishment that an airship was slowly descending upon my cow lot, about forty rods from the house.
>
> Calling my tenant, Gid Heslip, and my son Wall, we seized some axes and ran to the corral. Meanwhile, the ship had been gently descending until it was not more than thirty feet above the ground, and we came within fifty yards of it.
>
> It consisted of a great cigar-shaped portion, possibly three hundred feet long, with a carriage underneath. The carriage was made of glass or some other transparent substance alternating with a narrow strip of some material. It was brightly lighted within and everything was plainly visible – it was occupied by six of the strangest beings I ever saw. They were jabbering together but we could not understand a word they said.
>
> Every part of the vessel which was not transparent was of a dark reddish color. We stood mute with wonder and fright. Then some noise attracted their attention and they turned a light directly upon us. Immediately on catching sight of us they turned on some unknown power, and a great turbine wheel, about thirty feet in diameter, which was revolving slowly below the craft, began to buzz and the vessel rose lightly as a bird. When about three hundred feet above us it seemed to pause and to hover directly above a two-year-old heifer tangled in the wire fence. We tried to get it off but could not, so we cut the wire loose to see the ship, heifer and all, rise slowly, disappearing in the northwest.
>
> We went home but I was so frightened I could not sleep. Rising early Tuesday I started out on my horse, hoping to find some trace of my cow. This I failed to do, but coming back in the evening found that Link Thomas, about three or four miles west of LeRoy, had found the hide, legs, and head in his field that day.

He, thinking that someone had butchered a stolen beast, had brought the hide to town for identification, but was greatly mystified in not being able to find any tracks in the soft ground. After identifying the hide by my brand, I went home. But every time I would drop to sleep I would see the cursed thing, with its big lights and hideous people. I don't know whether they are devils or angels or what; but we all saw them, and my whole family saw the ship, and I don't want any more to do with them.

State of Kansas

Woodson County

As there are now, always have been, and always will be skeptics and unbelievers whenever the truth or anything bordering on the improbable is presented, and knowing that some ignorant or suspicious people will doubt the truthfulness of the above statement, now. Therefore we, the undersigned, do hereby make the following affidavit That we have known Alexander Hamilton from one to 30 years and that for truth and veracity we have never heard his word questioned and that we do verily believe his statement to be true and correct.

E. V. Wharton, State Oil Inspector
M. E. Hunt, Sheriff
H. H. Winter, Banker
E. K. Kellenberger, M.D.
H. S. Johnson, Pharmacist
J. H. Sticher, Attorney
Alexander Stewart, Justice of the Peace
H. Waymire, Druggist
F. W. Butler, Druggist
James L. Martin, Register of Deeds
H. D. Rollins, Postmaster
W. Lauber, Deputy Sheriff

Subscribed and sworn to me this 21st day of April 1897. W. C. Wille Notary Public. (Cohen, 1981: 93–5)

Of course, as with much of the airship mystery, this early cattle mutilation tale was undoubtedly nothing more than a newspaper hoax. As a matter of fact, the local dignitaries and upstanding citizens who swore an oath to vouch for Hamilton's character are reported to have been, with Hamilton, members in a local Liars Club, a common nineteenth-century establishment in which people would take turns making up the most outlandish tale they could imagine, only to be topped by the next teller of tall tales. Apparently Hamilton's story was so good the club decided to share it with the community, most of whom would have immediately recognized it for what it was.

From such simple and light-hearted beginnings has grown the strange and macabre world of cattle mutilation theory. As a tall tale from the nineteenth century it is almost charming. As a conspiracy theory for the twentieth century, filled with details of 'cored out' cattle rectums with holes the size of 'coffee cans,' it is another matter. The internet is filled with photos of these mutilations, rotting carcasses photographed in close-up and ready to be studied for information about beings from beyond the stars, like a sacrificed chicken studied for hints about the future or the will of the tribal gods. But in the case of cattle mutilations what is revealed in the divination is dark and foreboding – black helicopters from your own government supporting extraterrestrials in some sort of ritualistic slaughter of cattle. These divinations reveal beings that inspire neither fear nor wonder, only disgust and bewilderment.

◆ ◆ ◆

I don't know if this was meant as a joke or not, but as my faceless friends in the Mojave and I talked about extraterrestrial contacts, as people told their stories of lights in the sky or night time visitations, one of our party announced that there was an extraterrestrial in attendance at our conference. For a moment I did not know what to say. My first thought was to wonder why we were on a sky watch in the middle of the desert when there was an extraterrestrial back at our hotel. After thinking about it for a moment I asked the question aloud. 'If we want to know the secrets of time and space, if we want to receive the knowledge of the galaxy, why are we here when we could be having a face-to-face talk with an actual ET?'

'Because' one of my faceless friends informed me, 'she's a Tall White and if they don't like your looks they will gut you like a fish.'

That made sense to me.

She then proceeded to describe the woman in question. I recognized the description as fitting someone I had noticed earlier in the day. She was a very tall woman with very light skin and an awful lot of very blond hair. She wore dark glasses.

'That was a Tall White?' I said. 'I thought it was a guy in a dress.'

'Nope. Tall White. She confessed to someone in the buffet line at last year's conference.'

'Oh.'

I soon learned a lot about Tall Whites, including the fact that they sometimes try to pass as humans, just like our friend back in town, and are known to come out very late at night to prowl the streets of Las Vegas. It's always best to keep your distance from them, especially females with children. As my friend said, 'They're like mama bears. If they even suspect that you are a threat to one of their kids, they'll kill you instantly. You know they're fast for their size.'

'Oh, I know how fast aliens are,' I said, remembering how the baked potato outran the patrol car. 'I would definitely keep my distance if I ever had the chance to see one again.'

The existence of the Tall Whites was first revealed in Charles Hall's *Millennial Hospitality* (2002), a work described by the author as fictional, but based on true events. According to Hall's account, he worked as a weather observer at the Nellis Air Force Base from 1965 to 1966. His job required that he travel deep into the desert to monitor several weather stations. Previous incumbents in his position had reported strange events in the desert at night, including sightings of Range Four Harry, a mysterious white horse that was rumoured to have been exposed to radiation during atomic bomb tests many years before. Harry seemed to float above the ground and was able to inflict serious burns on anyone who got too close. Most of the previous weather observers had refused to go into the desert alone, falsifying weather records or deserting their posts. Hall, however, was different. He was able to maintain a relationship with Harry, actually one of many extraterrestrials who lived deep in the hills outside the airbase.

According to Hall, the Tall Whites are so called because that is exactly what they are. Averaging six or seven feet tall as adults, they are extremely pale and have large blue eyes. Their life span is much longer than ours, living approximately 800 years. They are well armed but dangerous even without their weaponry and over the course of their time at Nellis they have been involved in many incidents with military personnel. They explode with anger so suddenly and move so much more quickly than humans do that any time they feel threatened by humans a human is bound to die.

No one is sure when the Tall Whites arrived on earth, some saying in the Pre-Columbian period and some saying during the tenure of US President Madison. Hall notes that their caves resemble 1950s US construction. Hall theorized that earth may be a stopping point on some intergalactic trade route. In any event, the US government seems to be aware of the Tall Whites and even supportive of their continued residence in the Mojave. Perhaps, some suggest, the Tall Whites provide technological information to the military in exchange for some other commodity. Strangely enough, one of those commodities seems to be children's clothing.

Hall reports that the Tall White communities are filled with children and that their facilities invariably are equipped with playgrounds. In interviews Hall has stated that the US military supplies the Tall Whites with many of their necessities, including children's clothing. At least once, in the 1960s, the Air Force purchased over half a million dollars worth of children's clothing from Sears. In 1960s dollars, that was a lot of clothes, indicating that while some of the clothing may have been worn by Tall White children at Nellis, most of it must have been taken off-world. Perhaps the Tall Whites have discovered a market for children's clothing from Sears in some far distant, and polyester deprived, part of the galaxy.

At this point in my desert lesson I don't know whether to laugh or to cry. The whole story just seems so incongruous. Trading Sears clothing to the stars is one thing and floating around the desert at night ready to spring on any perceived threat with throat-ripping fury is another. And the government is involved in this, yet another conspiracy involving desert military bases and extraterrestrials? Was this in addition to what the government was doing at Area 51? Was this a different group of aliens to those that crashed at Roswell, or Aztec, or Aurora? If our government is trading for technology why go to all the trouble of reverse engineering bits of a saucer that didn't seem to have worked so well in the first place? I mean, it crashed didn't it? And what about the cows? Was it the miniature humanoids from Aztec or the grays from Roswell or the Tall Whites who carved up cattle in Alabama hill country? Very soon the world of UFO conspiracies begins to get very complicated. The Men in Black run together with the Tall Whites to produce a very murky shade of gray. My group of UFO watchers begins to get a little uncomfortable with all this talk. It's a little too dark and we are little too far out in the desert to be talking about Tall Whites. What if the Tall White representative spotted at the conference liked the climate out here in the desert? What is that ghostly white apparition off on the distant hills and what is that it is wearing? I think I had a shirt just like that when I was a kid, way back in the 1960s, probably bought on credit at a Sears department store . . .

4

Abductions

On October 16, 1957, very early in the morning, Antonio Villas Boas was plowing a field near Sao Francisco de Sales when he spotted a 'red star' in the pre-dawn sky. He realized that it was not an ordinary star when it rapidly grew larger and brighter, as if speeding in his direction. Soon he could make out the details of the light source. It was a circular or oval craft with a red light on the front and a spinning cupola on its top. The craft extended three legs and then proceeded to land in the freshly plowed field. Boas attempted to flee on his tractor, until the engine failed and the lights went dim. He then tried to flee on foot. Before he could get away he was seized by a human-like figure, some five feet tall, dressed in gray coveralls and a helmet. It had blue eyes that were smaller than normal human eyes. It did not speak any language that Boas could recognize but instead made strange barking noises. Three other similar creatures soon joined in forcing Boas aboard the craft.

Once inside, things started to get a little kinky. Boas was stripped of all of his clothes and then covered all over with a strange gel. He was taken to a large room where more of the beings took blood samples from his chin. He was then taken to a third room where he was left all alone for several minutes, perhaps as long as a half hour. At some point gas was pumped into the room, which made Boas feel terribly sick. After this another humanoid entered. (Now this is where it gets kinky.) Obviously of the same species as the others that Boas had encountered, this visitor was a woman. (I should add that this visitor was what Boas described as a very attractive, naked woman.) She stood at around the same height as her comrades, had a sharply pointed chin, blue 'cat-like' eyes, and long white hair. Since the being seemed to be as interested in him as he was in her, the two soon engaged in intercourse, during which the female did not kiss him but rather bit him rather violently on the chin and made the same kind of barking noises as her comrades.

After the affair was consummated, the woman gave Boas a big smile, rubbed her stomach, and pointed upward. Boas, now beginning to understand the situation a little better, interpreted this to mean that she was pregnant with his child and that she was going to give birth and raise him in outer space. According to Boas, the woman seemed relieved that her task was over and quickly left the room. Boas, who had at first been all for the idea of 'making it' with an alien, now felt a little used or, as he said, like a 'good stallion' for the aliens.

Boas was then allowed to dress and was given a brief tour of the craft. He was then deposited back on terra firma and watched the craft rise and disappear into the now bright morning sky. Back at home, Boas was shocked to find that four hours had elapsed. Time sure flies when you're having fun.

— Betty and Barney Hill —

While driving from Canada back to their home in Vermont, Betty and Barney Hill became the first victims of UFO abduction to achieve widespread popular recognition. While Boas's story did make it into a few tabloid newspapers, their story was told to the world in the best-selling book *The Interrupted Journey: Two Lost Hours 'Aboard a Flying Saucer'* (1965) by John G. Fuller. The book would inspire a made-for-TV movie and pave the way for the many accounts of alien abduction that were to follow. I remember watching the movie version of this story on television as a child and being absolutely terrified by it. James Earl Jones played the role of Barney and I was especially disturbed at seeing such a big man exhibit terror at the thought of what had happened to him. If he was afraid of the aliens, maybe I should be too. Suddenly, the Martians seemed even more threatening than before. They weren't just flying over in sport model saucers or fleeing at high speed from police officers.

UFO religion

They were actually taking people from their cars and performing strange experiments on them. While the earlier Boas story, which I did not hear until adulthood, was filled with good old-fashioned sex appeal that would have made many a young man wish to be abducted, the Hill story was just plain scary.

The Hills reported that during their late-night drive through deserted countryside they repeatedly spotted strange lights in the sky. On one occasion Barney left the car and walked across an open field to get a better view. In the field, near a vegetable patch and an old apple tree, Barney observed the craft through a pair of binoculars. From his vantage point he could see several windows on the craft and was able to distinguish humanoid figures leaning against them, as if to get a better look at him. The figures were wearing uniforms. The central figure was wearing a short brimmed hat.

> Then, on some invisible, inaudible signal, every member of the crew stepped back from the window toward a large panel a few feet behind the window line. Only one remained there looking at him, apparently a leader. In the binoculars, Barney could see appendages in action among the apparent crew at what seemed to be a control board behind the windows of the craft. (Fuller, 1965: 16)

The craft slowly descended a few feet at a time. Fins spread out from the sides of the craft, marked by blinking red lights. As the craft neared the ground something like a ladder was lowered from the underside.

> As the focus became sharp, he remembers the eyes of the one crew member who stared down at him. Barney had never seen eyes like that before. With all his energy he ripped the binoculars from his eyes and ran screaming back across the field to Betty and the car. (Fuller, 1965: 16–17)

Barney, as one might expect, was in a state of near hysteria.

For months afterward Betty and Barney struggled to make sense of their encounters, particularly with the fact that it seemed that there was more to the story than the sighting, something under the surface that they just could not remember. Then, through hypnosis, the rest of the story flooded their memories. The sightings had only been the beginning of their experience. From their repressed memories they discovered that they had actually been taken aboard the alien vessel and subjected to strange examinations. Betty describes part of her experience in the following way:

> So I'm sitting on the stool, and there's a little bracket, my head is resting against this bracket. And the examiner opens my eyes, and looks in them with a light, and he opens my mouth, and he looks in my throat and my teeth and he looks in my ears, and he turned my head, and he looked in this ear . . . Oh, and then he feels my hair down by the back of my neck and all, and they take a couple of strands of my hair, and they pull it out, and he gives this to the leader and he wraps that all up and puts that in the top drawer . . . (Fuller, 1965: 160–1)

Later, Betty was rolled over on her back. The examiners approached her with a long needle that was inserted in her navel. Though the procedure initially caused her a great amount of pain, the pain subsided after the leader rubbed his hand in front of her eyes. When Betty asked them the purpose of the procedure they told her it was a pregnancy test. Having completed similar tests on Barney they were both apparently placed back in their car and made to forget the incident. It was only after they arrived at home in the morning that they realized that the trip had taken two hours longer than it should have and that they had no memory of an entire stretch of the journey.

In telling their story, Fuller presents what he believes are the conclusions that can be drawn from their testimony. First, Fuller insists that a sighting 'of some sort' took place. Second, the sighting was of a craft. Third, whatever happened, Betty and Barney Hill had severe emotional reactions to it. Fourth, the emotional intensity of the event was amplified by Barney's sensitivity to the fact that he was a black man married to a white woman. Fifth, Fuller says that the Hills had no ulterior motives to make up such an outlandish story. Indeed, for four years they had told only their closest family and friends about the event. Sixth, the case was investigated by several technical and scientific persons. Seventh, there is physical evidence that supports the Hills' claims, including marks on the trunk of their car, the strange behavior of a compass held in the vicinity of the marks, the fact that the Hills' watches malfunctioned after the night in question, and Barney's broken binoculars. Finally, under hypnosis the Hills told nearly identical stories. In response to these facts, Fuller writes

> [I]f it can even momentarily be speculated that the event is true, the far-reaching implications concerning the history of the world are obvious.
>
> Such an event would demand a reexamination of religion, politics, science, and even literature. (Fuller, 1965: 295)

Is Fuller's evidence really all that conclusive? I can think of a lot of ulterior motives someone might have for making up such a story; broken watches hardly seem like conclusive evidence that the Hills were abducted; and I'm not really that confident in the powers of hypnotherapy to recover facts about actual events. Likewise his concluding point seems a bit overblown. I don't even know what it means to say that 'if it can even momentarily be speculated that the event is true . . .' It seems that it would take a lot more than momentarily speculating that something might be true to overturn religion, politics, science, and *even* literature. Plus, there's that drawing of the alien leader made by Barney in which the alien is wearing a hat like the one worn by Marlon Brando in *Rebel Without a Cause* (or was it *The Wild One*)? What is that about? I can't believe this stuff scared me as child. Even more strangely, I can't believe that it still scares me today.

I don't mean that I am literally scared that I might be abducted by extraterrestrials and subjected to experiments. No, the Hills' story frightens me in a far more primitive way. It makes the same tingle go up my spine that accompanies déjà vu. Hearing their tale gives me the same feeling I have when I awake from a dream, unable to remember its content, but with my bloodstream awash in adrenaline. Because the Hills' abduction experience takes place in the space between dreaming and wakefulness, its facts only brought to light under hypnosis, it has a nightmarish quality only strengthened by the fuzziness of the details and the absurdity of the claims. An alien dressed like Marlon Brando, now that's creepy!

— Betty Andreasson —

Betty Andreasson's encounter with alien abductors occurred not on a lonely stretch of highway but in her own home, surrounded by family. Betty's abductors entered her home by passing through the door. The aliens, dressed in military-style uniforms, seemed to have placed Betty's family in a state of suspended animation, for they stood silent and motionless as the drama unfolded. As with the Hills, Betty's experience came back to her in detail only while in a state of hypnosis. The record of Betty's hypnosis sessions is recounted in Raymond Fowler's 1979 book, *The Andreasson Affair: The Documented Investigation of a Woman's Abduction Aboard a UFO*. The record of Betty's testimony under hypnosis with annotations by Fowler includes a description of her first interaction with the visitors.

> The leader stretched out his hand, and [Betty] asked, 'Do you want something to eat?' [The visitors] merely nodded.
>
> BETTY: And so I went and got some food from the refrigerator and a pan from the stove, and I started to cook some meat.
>
> The entities stared impassively at Betty momentarily, and then she received another mental impression:
>
> BETTY: And I turned, because they said something to me. And they said, 'We cannot eat food unless it is burned.' And so I started to burn the meat – and they stepped back, astonished over the smoke that was coming up!
>
> The beings corrected Betty as clearer images formed in her mind:
>
> BETTY: And they said, 'But that's not our kind of food. Our food is tried by fire, knowledge tried by fire. Do you have any food like that?'
>
> Betty's religious beliefs influenced her reply: 'Yes, I think I have some like that . . . It's in there.' . . .
>
> BETTY: They followed me into the living room, and I looked and I saw all my family as if time had stopped for them. And I wondered what happened. But I glanced down and picked up the Bible that was on the end table. I turned and passed it to the leader. The leader passed me a little thin book in exchange. (Fowler, 1979: 27–8)

UFO religion

Betty Andreasson's encounter with the aliens in her kitchen is reminiscent of stories from Jewish and Christian scriptures, and is especially similar in tone to some passages from the Gospel of John and the Book of Revelation. Like the disciples with Jesus, Betty fails to understand that the visitor is referring to spiritual matters rather than purely physical nourishment when he talks of food. Such religious allusions are a common theme in Betty's testimony and in her description of being taken on board an alien craft, undergoing an examination similar to that of Betty and Barney Hill, being transported to the alien realm, and returning to her home. Betty makes it clear that she was taken by the aliens, not simply to another planet, but to another reality.

DAVID: Were you taken to their home planet?
BETTY: (Long pause and weak voice) I was taken to the high place, higher than their home planet.
DAVID: You mean a more important planet?
BETTY: It is not a planet, it is a place.

The religious allusions in Betty's testimony are frequently associated with ethical teachings or warnings.

Betty was then returned to a hypnotic state and was asked if the aliens had anything to do with a recent power blackout in New York City.
BETTY: They have powers. They can control the wind, and water and even lightning.
DAVID: Did they tell you what the purpose of the blackout was?
BETTY: It was to reveal to man his true nature.
DAVID: What is man's true nature?
BETTY: Man seeks to destroy himself. Greed, greed, greed, greed. And because of greed, it draws all foul things. Everything has been provided for man. Simple things. He could be advanced so far, but greed gets in the way. Freely it will be given to those who love.
(Betty speaks in a strange tongue.)
FRED: Betty is this message for us?
A feeling of tension filled the crowded office as again Betty's face became twisted and words forced themselves out through her reluctant lips.
BETTY: Even – now – you – cannot – see. Even – now – we – speak.

DAVID: We are trying to see. Do you have a message for us?
BETTY: You – try – to – seek – in – wrong – directions. – Simplicity – 'round about you. – Air – you breathe – water – you drink – (sigh) – fire – that – warms – earth – that – heals. – Simplicity ashes – things – that – are – necessary – taken – for – granted. – Powers – within them – overlooked. – Why – think – you – are able – to live? Simplicity. (Fowler, 1979: 146 and 140–1)

In this particular example Betty exhibits the gift of glossalallia, or speaking in tongues, a gift reported as accompanying the anointing of the Holy Spirit in the Christian Acts of the Apostles. This is followed by ethical teachings, limited though they may be, that encourage humans to seek a simpler way of life and to learn to appreciate the truly important elements of our existence – earth, air, fire, and water. One wonders why aliens would deliver a message to Betty Andreasson and then cloud her memory so that she could only remember it under hypnosis. One also wonders if this rather pedestrian bit of ethical teaching is all that the aliens have to offer.

Despite the fact that the didactic payoff to the Andreasson affair is such a letdown, the religious allusions throughout the tale serve to make Betty Andreasson's abduction account stand out from the stories that came before it, however. There wasn't much sex in the tale but there is a lot of high weirdness, including an encounter with a mythical phoenix while visiting the alien realm. I have to say that there is something about this strange mixture of alien abduction and Christian mythology that, though making it no easier to believe in, nevertheless makes it a bit more unsettling. But then again I've already confessed that my childhood fear of UFOs was equaled only by my childhood fear of Jesus. Betty Andreasson hits me with a double blow.

— The Allagash Abductions —

Raymond Fowler followed up his account of Betty Andreasson with *The Allagash Abductions: Undeniable Evidence of Alien Intervention* (1993), the story of the 1976 abduction experiences of Charlie Foltz, Chuck Rak, and twins Jim and Jack Weiner. The four men reported to Fowler, under hypnosis, that their 1976 trip down the Allagash River was marked by a strange encounter. The men reported that while fishing at night on a deserted stretch of river they observed a bright light hovering over the trees that then proceeded to approach their boat. The men remembered being very afraid and then suddenly finding themselves back on the riverbank. The huge fire they had built earlier was burned down to coals, indicating that they had been on the river far longer than was possible. For years after the event the men experienced strange dreams that only became clear as their memories were freed during the hypnotic regression sessions. In the time between the first sighting of the UFO and their arrival back on shore, in the missing period of time from their memories, the men had been taken aboard the alien craft and subjected to strange physical examinations.

Fowler finds that one of the most compelling reasons to take the account as truth is that the men agreed on many details of the account even though they had sworn not to talk with each other between hypnotic sessions. For example, all four men agreed in the basic details of the aliens' appearance. In the description of the aliens' heads:

> JIM: Their heads are egg-shaped.
> JACK: Large round heads . . . nothing on top.
> CHARLIE: The head is . . . like egg-shaped . . . No hair.
> CHUCK: Looks like an embryonic chicken head . . . Cranium almost looks like a duck . . . bulbous . . . Can't see hair.

eyes:

> JIM: Bugging-looking eyes . . . They're dark . . . Temporally located.
> JACK: Large eyes on the sides of their heads . . . Funny-looking . . . like eggs.
> CHARLIE: Like large Asian, almond eyes.
> CHUCK: Dark eyes . . . elliptical. They're black.

mouth, nose, ears:

> JIM: Something like a mouth . . . They don't have ears, just, ah, holes . . . They don't have noses, there's something, ah, there.

JACK:	Like turtle mouths . . . no nose . . . no ears.
CHARLIE:	They don't have like a mouth – like if your lips were sealed . . . An Asian nose . . . small compared to mine – ears smaller . . . lays close.
CHUCK:	(The mouth is) like chicken lips . . . Can't really make it (the nose) out . . . Can't really see much . . . (of the ears) just suggested.

and body build:

JIM:	Bony . . . an exoskeleton.
JACK:	They're small and thin. I can't see their joints . . . Thin . . . arms
CHARLIE:	Slight build . . . petite.
CHUCK:	They're bony . . . slender. (Fowler, 1993: 326, 327 and 328)

Unfortunately, Fowler offers no proof that the men haven't planned their testimony ahead of time or, even without malice, been influenced by discussions of each others' dreams during the long interval between the event and the hypnosis sessions.

What strikes me about the Allagash abductions is not the evidence for the veracity of the accounts, but the sense in reading Fowler's book that the men were truly afraid of something. I'm not sure that we have any more reason to think that their fear was generated by an actual encounter with extraterrestrials than that it was the result of any number of other things. The men all seem to have been terrified for years without any real sense of why they were afraid or what they were afraid of. The actual abduction narrative is, in this sense, less powerful than their fear of the unknown, so that it almost seems that the encounter with extraterrestrials is an attempt to incarnate the unknown or the unthinkable, a safer alternative than the truth, perhaps. It's like those old horror movies that were scary right up until the time that the monster was finally revealed. Once you had seen the cheap rubber costume with a zipper on the back the fear was all gone. It was the unknowing anticipation that offered the real terror.

— Whitley Streiber —

The extraterrestrials as detailed in *The Allagash Abductions* are usually described as Grays, to distinguish them from the diminutive but human-like aliens of the Aztec crash, the monstrous beings of Bender and Barker, and other reported types. Grays, sounding an awful lot like the aliens in Steven Spielberg's *Close Encounters of the Third Kind*, became most clearly identified with abduction tales in 1988's *Communion* by science-fiction writer Whitley Streiber. The alien pictured on the cover of Streiber's bestseller has become the iconic image of earth's alien visitors. Indeed, Streiber and at least one other leading abduction researcher, Budd Hopkins, seem to have recognized the importance of the cover illustration even before the book went to print. According to the May 2006 issue of *Saucer Smear*, published by longtime saucerian Jim Moseley, Hopkins was in contact with Streiber during the writing and publication of the book. Moseley writes:

> [Hopkins] was in frequent touch with Whitley Strieber in 1986 when Strieber's best-selling 'Communion' book was being written. Strieber hired an artist to faithfully reproduce the exact facial features of the 'Gray' aliens he had been seeing. Finally, the book and the cover painting were finished, and Strieber told Hopkins by phone that 'the painting is uncanny. It is *exactly* (emphasis added) like the faces I have seen.' Strieber was very excited about this fact, and raved on at length about his satisfaction with the artist's rendition. However, when Hopkins actually saw the painting, he was 'shocked and profoundly disappointed'. In Hopkins' opinion, there was a 'staggering error' The cranium was much too small, virtually a pinhead, and the hypnotically staring eyes were so close to the top of the head that the result was 'grotesque' – like a carnival freak. Egads! He told Whitley, 'The aliens are universally described as having huge craniums, not little pinheads like this.' Strieber quickly agreed. He said, 'Now that I think about it, I remember that yes, they did have big heads'.

Streiber's account of his own experiences, though undergoing a great number of changes throughout the years, provided more than the prototype of the image of alien abductor, however. It also provided one of the most well-known versions of the abduction experience itself, with a narrative structure that would appear in many other abduction accounts.

This is not to say that Streiber's tale does not contain elements unique to his own case. For example, his description of the interior of the spacecraft is markedly different to the usual description of the interior as a cold, sterile environment.

> The small, circular chamber had a domed, grayish-tan ceiling with ribs appearing at intervals of about a foot. I had an impression that it was messy, a living space. Across the room to my right some clothing was thrown on the floor. As a matter of fact, the thought even crossed my mind that the place was actually dirty. It was close and confining for me. The whole scale of it was small, tight, and enclosed. I seem to remember that the room was stuffy and the air quite dry, so it could be that the numbness of panic was wearing off.
>
> Tiny people were now moving around me at great speed. Their quickness was disturbing, and in a curious way ugly. . . .

In most cases, however, Streiber's experience mirrors that of Betty and Barney Hill and others. There is, for example, a bench along the wall on which Streiber sits.

> Despite my extreme terror, I was aware of my surroundings. I know that I was seated on a bench, leaning against a wall. The predominant colors were tan and gray. The bench was the same color as the walls, and was rimmed by a lip of dark brown . . .

There was also a surgical procedure involving a needle.

> My memory of the one that came before me next is of a tiny, squat person, crouching as if huddled over something. He had been given [a] box and now slid it open, revealing an extremely shiny, hair-thin needle mounted on a black surface. This needle glittered when I saw it out of the corner of my eye, but was practically invisible straight on.
>
> I became aware – I think I was told – that they proposed to insert this into my brain. (Streiber, 1987: 16, 17 and 18)

We should also note that Streiber's narrative includes a diversity of alien types – his front-cover alien being one of four 'species' encounters on the spacecraft.

> The first was the small robot like being that had led the way into
> my bedroom. He was followed by a large group of short, stocky
> ones in the dark-blue overalls. These had wide faces, appearing
> either dark gray or dark blue in that light, with glittering deep-
> set eyes, pug noses, and broad, somewhat human mouths. Inside
> the room, I encountered two types of creature that did not look
> at all human. The most provocative of these was about five feet
> tall, very slender and delicate, with extremely prominent and
> mesmerizing black slanted eyes. This being had an almost vestig-
> ial mouth and nose. The huddled figures in the theater were
> somewhat smaller, with similarly shaped heads but round, black
> eyes, like large buttons. (Streiber, 1987: 20)

The veracity of the strange events related by Streiber are continually undercut in *Communion* by descriptions of his reactions to
these event that make one think, not of the reactions a person would
have to bizarre happenings but rather reactions a person would
have to a dream. For example, Streiber describes his reactions on one
particular night:

> In the middle of the night on December 26 – I do not know the
> exact time – I abruptly found myself awake. And I knew why: I
> heard a peculiar whooshing, swirling noise coming from the liv-
> ing room downstairs. This was no random creak, no settling of
> the house, but a sound as if a large number of people were mov-
> ing rapidly around in the room. . . .
> What I did next may seem peculiar. I settled back in bed. For
> some reason the extreme strangeness of what I was hearing did
> not rouse me to action. Over the course of this narrative this sort
> of inappropriate response will be repeated many times. If some-
> thing is strange enough, the reaction is very different from what
> one might think. The mind seems to tune it out as if by some sort
> of instinct. (Streiber, 1987: 11)

I suppose that Streiber's explanation for the fact that he settled
back in bed offers one possible explanation for his behavior. It seems
to me, however, that Streiber reacted the way one normally reacts
when awakened by a dream. Streiber's own confession of the inap-
propriateness of his response to these strange circumstances only
reinforces my impression that perhaps Streiber is not a victim of
alien abductions but rather is an individual with a very healthy
dream life. That is just the sort of thing you would expect to find in

a science-fiction writer. Of course, that is an experience that can be terrifying all by itself, even without any little gray men.

— The Reproductive Agenda —

In the writings of Budd Hopkins, alien abduction experiences have taken on a decidedly reproductive theme. Indeed, in *Sight Unseen* he and his co-writer Carol Rainey, have argued that the reproductive element has been a part of abductions from the beginning, though it has often been ignored because of the squeamishness of researchers and audiences. I don't know if the pun is intended or not when Hopkins and Rainey refer to the Betty and Barney Hill experience as the 'seminal' case of UFO abductions, but they seem very serious when they claim that in that early case the reproductive agenda of the aliens was already on display. The first hint of this is found in the 'pregnancy test' administered to Betty. Another hint is found in a part of the story that was not included in Fuller's published account. Not only was Betty given a pregnancy test but extraterrestrials extracted a sperm sample from Barney. They write:

> Later abduction accounts and the analysis of many case studies suggest that the aliens 'needle-in-the-navel' procedures were not tests to determine if a woman is pregnant but might actually have been ova-retrieval operations and thus exactly analogous to commonly reported sperm-sampling operations such as the one Barney Hill underwent. (Hopkins and Rainey, 2003: 166–7)

Hopkins reports, based on details from abductee testimonies, that the reproductive agenda of our alien visitors goes far beyond pregnancy tests and sperm samples, however. Hopkins claims that in 'hundreds' of cases women report being abducted and artificially inseminated, a procedure that results in a pregnancy. The pregnancy usually lasts to the end of the first trimester and then disappears with no evidence of the pregnancy to be found. 'In one case, an abductee who is by profession an obstetrical nurse had her fetus disappear in the fifth month, and though she passed the fetal sac and experienced some bleeding, she was disturbed to find that there was no actual fetal tissue' (Hopkins and Rainey, 2003: 168).

Furthermore, in 'scores of cases' investigated by Hopkins, female abductees report reabductions some months or years following the pregnancy. They are then shown an infant or toddler that they feel to be their own lost child. The aliens frequently seem to want the women to hold and bond with the children. After a short while the child is taken from the woman, who is then returned to the place from where she was abducted.

> These children – who, for want of a better term, I call 'hybrids' – are described by the abductees as showing a mix of alien and human characteristics. Often the eyes are quite large and either blue or almost entirely black. They usually have thin, wispy, white-blond hair that does not seem to evenly cover their scalp. Their noses are small or nearly non-existent, their lips are thin, and their heads often overly large. Though they have not often been naked when they were presented, on those exceptional occasions abductees have noticed that the children seemed to lack navels. (Hopkins and Rainey, 2003: 171)

Fellow abduction researcher David M. Jacobs further details the experience of women who are reabducted and reunited with their 'lost' children. In *Secret Life* (1992), Jacobs reports that abductees sometimes report being taken to what he calls the 'incubatorium.' The woman is then shown fetuses incubating inside some strange apparatus. Sometimes the fetuses are positioned upright floating in a liquid environment or lying down, sometimes in liquid and sometimes in dry environments (Jacobs, 1992: 153). Often, when the reabduction takes place some time after the pregnancy women are taken not to an incubatorium but to a nursery. The nursery sometimes houses as many as a hundred babies, with the babies lying in beds in multiple rows. Most frequently they are in transparent boxes. The babies usually appear phlegmatic and sickly (Jacobs, 1992: 162).

Jacobs, like Hopkins, reports that the women are often instructed to interact with the children. Though the women are usually exposed to babies they are sometimes presented with young children and, occasionally, adolescents. According to Jacobs this seems to indicate that the children are in need of human contact. Sometimes the instructions from the alien abductors are quite explicit.

The woman hears another directive: 'Nurse the baby.' 'Put the baby to your breast and feed the baby.' The woman says, 'But I do not have any milk.' The response is 'Put the baby to your breast and nurse the baby!' Saying 'No' is futile. If she resists, the aliens will put the baby to her breast anyway. It cups its mouth on her nipple. It has a very weak sucking reflex. In many instances, the woman may be surprised to find that she is lactating and that her breasts are engorged. When that happens the baby will partially drain the breast. Often, however, nursing the baby is futile but seems to satisfy the watchful aliens nonetheless. (Jacobs, 1992: 174)

In addition to the already objectionable practice of using earth women to incubate human alien hybrids through kidnapping and artificial insemination, Jacobs also reports instances where the abductee is actually raped, apparently for the purpose of acquiring a fertilized egg. He reports the experience of a fifteen-year-old girl who was forced into intercourse by an older man.

[I]t feels like he starts to climax and doesn't finish, or he gets to the point of coming, but what's the point of that? What's the point of that? . . . They just pull him off, and they stick something up where he was, a metal thing it feels like. And then they're moving very fast. . . .

She described how the Beings apparently took an egg from her at this point and they then walked the man away.

Girls are often abducted during puberty, according to Jacobs. They report being examined by the aliens and told that they are now fertile and that they should 'go and breed.'

When one woman was thirteen, the aliens told her this, and then, as if to show her how it is done, they brought in a teenage boy who seemed to be 'out of it' and put him on top of her so that intercourse could be accomplished. Afterward, she felt pain and noticed blood on her legs. Her hymen had been ruptured. This was done at least one other time to her when she was a teenager.

Finally, Jacobs reports that women are often forced to have intercourse with alien/human hybrids. According to his research:

The insertion of the 'penis' is quick, and the penis does not feel normal; it is usually very thin and very short. The normal thrusting movement does not take place, but the woman feels a sudden 'pulse.' Then it is all over. We have no clear evidence that the aliens have genitals, but hybrids sometimes do. (Jacobs, 1992: 205 and 206)

The many elements of these female abductees' experiences point to a reproductive agenda on the part of the aliens. Why would visitors from another planet have abducted thousands of earth people over the course of, at least, the last fifty years? Why would they continually subject those abductees to reproductive examinations? Both Hopkins and Jacobs believe that they have found the answer in the testimony of the women they have interviewed. The alien species must be on the verge of genetic collapse. They are in need of new genetic material to strengthen their species, which may have become so technologically and mentally advanced that their bodies have atrophied. Human genetic material would provide them with the rejuvenated gene pool they so desperately need. Or, perhaps the aliens are attempting to infiltrate earth society by cross-breeding with humans until they are free to blend into our culture and remain unnoticed. Either way, these activities are dark and sinister. Human girls and women are abused for the purposes of some mysterious alien agenda. This is a far cry from the notion that earth governments have captured flying saucers and used the technology found therein to protect the earth from an alien menace. In this scenario the aliens are prowling our neighborhoods at night, looking to abduct earth women for their own evil schemes, and there seems to be nothing that anyone can do about it.

Okay, now I am beginning to get really scared again. And once again it is not because I am afraid that I might be abducted by an alien. (I'm actually hoping for a retro abduction that includes short, barking, white-haired alien girls.) No, I'm beginning to get scared because what Hopkins and Jacobs have to say is pretty creepy stuff. I think I'll get on my 'high horse' for a moment and say that the theories of an alien reproductive agenda, complete with rape and pedophilia, are just a little more than I can stomach. On the flimsiest of evidence, testimony derived from individuals while under hypnosis, Hopkins and Jacobs are prepared to confirm to women that their worst nightmares, rape and the kidnapping of their children, are real. Maybe this doesn't so much scare me, as make me sick.

Whether these accounts are real or not, the individuals involved would seem to need more help than either Hopkins or Jacobs are qualified to offer.

— Creative Transformation —

In contrast to the theories of Hopkins and Jacobs, John E. Mack saw the alien abduction phenomenon in what was primarily a positive light. In his 1994 book *Abduction: Human Encounter with Aliens*, his experiences as a therapist who treated abductees had led him to believe that the aliens are involved in two related projects. First, they are attempting to change human consciousness and behavior to prevent the destruction of life on earth. Second, they are attempting to join our two species in the creation of a new, and better, third species.

Their interest in the earth no doubt springs from the fact that the earth is an integral part of the cosmic system. Problems on earth may impact the balance of life on many other worlds and in many other realities. The abduction phenomenon may be an attempt to correct some of earth's problems before they cause damage to the cosmic system as a whole. In support of this theory Mack offers the testimony of 'Anne,' an abductee.

> Anne . . . learned from her experiences that 'the whole universe is self-correcting, because if one part of the universe can be . . . like a feedback machine, the whole thing has to be self-correcting like a feedback machine.' She likened the universe to a tapestry. 'It's all connected. If you take one part of the tapestry, and you put a hole in it or you rend it, you wreck the parts that are next to it. If you take a thread out, the threads that are next to it all get bumped and jostled about so you've got to correct it . . . If you make a mess in one part of the universe,' she continued, 'you jostle the next part over, and the part that's able to move in or adjust will do so.' (Mack, 1994: 412)

According to Mack, almost all abductees are given information concerning the destruction of the earth's environment. The experience of the abductees is, however, more than just the reception of information, they also experience a change in consciousness in regards to the issue and desire to make changes for the better. He writes:

> Abductees experience powerful images of vast destruction, with the collapse of governmental and economic infrastructures and the total pollution and desertification of the planet. ... I have been greatly moved as they sob on the couch and experience heartache so intense that they can barely bring themselves to speak of it. ... Writer and futurist Jean Houston, at the Congress of the World Parliament of Religions in Chicago in September 1993, commented that all myths begin with a form of betrayal. Perhaps the human betrayal of the earth itself is giving rise to a new myth of interspecies relationship and creation. (Mack, 1994: 412–13)

In part because of this important message that is being transmitted to abductees, Mack believes that the aliens must be more than evil scientists or rapists. If their actions are in any way related to their message, then they must be seeking, through the abduction phenomenon and through the reproductive agenda, to bring about some positive change. Mack believed that this attempt at an 'awkward joining of two species' is intended for the good of both humans and aliens. Many abductees come away from their experiences with the feeling that the interaction between the two species is meant for the good of both. Often, abductees describe the visitors as seeming to be closer to the source of creation in the universe. They are attempting to show us the way to strengthen our spiritual selves. Or, as Mack describes it, 'Through their interaction with the abductees they bring them (and all of us potentially) closer to our spiritual cosmic roots, return us to the divine light or "Home," a "place" (really a state of being) where secrets, jealousy, greed, and destructiveness have no purpose' (Mack, 1994: 413–14).

While doing this the aliens are clearly seeking something that they can gain from us, but perhaps it is more than the physical strength and hardiness that some see them seeking. Perhaps it is that they have become emotionally empty because of their separation from their embodiment. Like 'love-starved children', they long to experience the embodiedness of human existence through us. They wish to open the world of the spirit to us and to reclaim the world of the flesh through us. Sometimes, says Mack, 'abductees even develop a deep love and affection for the alien beings. . . . The experience can be one of profound, total, even blissful merging. Some abductees have experienced actual alien–human sexual connection or partnership' (1994: 415).

I don't know. Sounds like Stockholm Syndrome to me.

◆ ◆ ◆

If I had to choose the type of abduction I would want, the choice would be obvious. While I am plowing a field an egg suddenly drops from the sky. The crew of the egg takes me aboard and forces me to 'do it' with a really cute alien girl. Then I am unceremoniously dumped and the girl is never to be seen again. Wham, bam, etc. Now that would be a great abduction experience. Alas, as far as I know there has been only one such experience reported. If I am abducted, chances are it won't turn out so well.

Most abduction narratives are strikingly different from the one reported by Antonio Villas Boas. Though they do share a common sexual element, the tone of the sexual encounters is darker in the later stories. This is not surprising, for those stories are are all about fear and trembling, all about awe before the unknown. Sometimes it is the kind of fear and trembling one might experience before strange lights in the night sky or the starry heavens above; the kind of fear and trembling that we all have in the face of the unknown, before the mysteries of our almost-forgotten dreams; the kind of fear and trembling that is elicited by the reality of our own vulnerability. Sometimes it is the kind of childish fear and trembling one might have before a tin-foil alien, the fear of strange sounds in the night, the lurking menace in the closet, or the shuffle under your bed.

I know these fears and I bet you do too. Sometimes before I go to sleep at night I think to myself how foolish it is for all of us, practically every human being for thousands of miles in every direction, to go to sleep at the same time. As if locked doors could provide us the protection we need from the kinds of things that don't sleep when we sleep, the kinds of things that go bump in the night, the kind of things about which we dare not speak. Of course there are also the other kinds of fears, fears that the tales of alien abduction bring out into the open. These tales reveal our fears of things unspeakable, our fears of rape and loss and abuse and the other, oh so real, terrors of human life.

Unfortunately, these very real fears are often treated by the 'experts' in the field of alien abduction with a creepiness somewhere between that of a pimply faced teenage boy and a dirty old man. For them it is all about little guys who want to stick things in our wangs and wahoos, medical doctors from Planet X; oh my God, they've stripped me naked! Colonel Shaw taught us way back in 1897 that these guys are no match for a good strong resident of planet earth. Even Hopkins and Jacobs seem to think of the grays as weak and wilted, in desperate need of a good dose of DNA from good old earth. So why should we find these guys so threatening? If women are being raped and if their babies are being taken from their wombs, then these women need more help than people like Hopkins and Jacobs can give them. This is likewise true if these are subjective rather than objective experiences. For the latter they need help from trained professionals, for the former they need the FBI or, better yet, the MIB.

Ah, Antonio, you don't know how good you had it.

PART TWO

Contactees

5

Scout Ships from Venus

I prepared for my trip to the California desert by carefully mapping my route through the towns of Joshua Tree and Landers to my destination, Giant Rock – home of the first UFO contactee conventions. I had even examined satellite images of the route before leaving home, zooming in as close as possible to the giant rock itself, thinking that my view from above, courtesy of satellite photography and internet information sharing, must be something like the view from a flying saucer. I put all of that preparation aside, however, when between Joshua Tree and Landers I passed a road marked 'Giant Rock Road.' Maps or no maps, satellite imagery or no satellite imagery, this had to be the way.

It wasn't.

Giant Rock Road turned out to be a mostly unimproved trail that led past a few modest homes and then extended on into the distant desert. At one point I passed a rusted and derelict pickup truck. Most of it was missing, the rusty shell looked like the remains of something long dead, its bones picked clean by some huge scavenger bird. I was here to search the skies for flying saucers but some more primal instinct made me look up for any signs of a buzzard big enough to devour my rental car. Coast clear, I drove on and found myself even more lost.

Hidden behind a mesa I found a fenced compound filled with old automobiles, a couple of shacks, and a lot of dogs. I kept on driving. Finally I managed to flag down a motorcyclist who informed me that I was a very long way from Giant Rock.

'Can you tell me how to get there?' I asked.

'Sure,' he answered. 'But not by road and I'm not sure your car can make it over the rough terrain.'

'I'll give it a try', I said, trying to sound as if I knew what I was doing.

He pointed to a pass between two hills in the far distance. 'Just keep driving toward that pass,' he said. 'Ignore the roads. You can't miss it.'

There was no way I was going to 'ignore the roads' so I thanked him and proceeded to retrace my steps back to the main road. In thirty minutes or so I was back to civilization, if by civilization one means a two-lane black-top roadway in the middle of nowhere. This time I would not be fooled by misleading road signs. I would follow my map.

I found Giant Rock right where my map said it would be, just a short drive across the open desert from the small town of Landers, California. I don't know what I was expecting with a name like 'Giant Rock' but I was surprised by how, oh, let's say 'gigantic,' the rock really was. The rock, sitting on the ground at the foot of a large mesa is the size of a seven-story building and makes quite an impression. Other than its size, the first thing I noticed was that a large portion of the rock had broken off and fallen to the ground. I had read about the break a few years earlier and knew that it was taken by some to be an indication that a major event was about to take place. Some even claimed that Native American prophecy had predicted that the rock would split as a sign that the end of the world was near. The lower part of giant rock, to the height that was easily reachable by standing on the ground, was filled with graffiti, some of it in the form of crudely painted flying saucers and extraterrestrials. I could see that the earth under the rock had been removed and that a large number of rabbits called the hollow home. Adjacent to the rock I found a small concrete slab, also decorated by grafitti, in this case by a listing of the planets in our solar system from Mercury to Pluto. The ground around the rock was littered with debris, including a set of rusted bed springs placed neatly against the back side of the rock, as if someone still slept on them, bare metal, rust, and all, perhaps a member of some austere religious order that, instead of flagellation and fasting, required its members to sleep in the desert on a bed of rust.

I closed my eyes and tried to imagine the way it was in the 1950s. The rock had been whole, its underside fit for humans to explore and even camp. (During World War II the cave underneath had been used as a home for a prospector who, because of his German-sounding last name, was killed in an encounter with local police. Apparently, or so the story goes, a stray bullet from an officer's gun ignited the prospector's dynamite, killing the unfortunate fellow as a result.) The concrete slab had been the foundation of a burger shack. Nearby, two airplanes sat on a desert runway. There were people everywhere, straining their ears to hear the voice of the speaker . . .

> The speaker's makeshift platform stood high against Giant Rock itself. The interminable preparations came to an end and George Van Tassel climbed up to speak. Shortly, he was heard to say, 'Yes, we are here. Who am I talking to?'
> For several minutes listeners heard only a one-sided conversation. 'NOW who am I talking to? Well, somebody else keeps butting in! CONFOUND IT, YOU KEEP SWITCHING AROUND ON ME! Let's settle on who is to do the talking tonight!'
> Suddenly, Van Tassel began speaking in a loud, harsh voice which identified itself as 'Knut'.
> 'I AM KNUT. I BRING YOU LOVE.'
> Knut proceeded to tell the assembled party that he was stationed in a '300 foot supply ship, approximately 200 miles to the south, and 5260 feet high'. When the group stepped outside to look for this miraculous craft, they were rewarded with nothing more than the beauty of the desert night and a few shooting stars. (Gregory Bishop and Kenn Thomas, 'The Giant Rock Conventions,' *Fortean Times*, January 1999: 118)

In those days George Van Tassel channeled messages from extraterrestrial entities from his position underneath Giant Rock, including instructions concerning the construction of the Integratron in nearby Landers. When Van Tassel organized contactee conventions, starting in 1954 at his runway and hamburger stand at Giant Rock thousands of people came to tell their stories and listen to the stories of others. In 1954 the list of speakers included Orfeo Agnelucci, Truman Bethurum, Daniel Fry, and George Hunt Williamson. These individuals, and many more like them, made claims that were far more startling than any claim to have seen strange

6. *Saucer refueling station in Rachel, Nevada. No indication of the price of saucer fuel*

lights in the sky or to have handled the wreckage from a downed flying saucer. They were part of what was derisively called the 'lunatic fringe' by those in the 'nuts and bolts' UFO communities, and they claimed not only to have seen extraterrestrials and their crafts but to have had contact with such beings and taken rides in their flying saucers. They came away from these contacts with messages for mankind, at least in one case about the need for changes in the human diet, but most of the time with messages of world peace, human brotherhood, and the need for love and kindness. These were the contactees.

— Theosophy —

Just as the sources for twentieth-century flying saucer sightings can be traced back to the late nineteenth century so can the sources for twentieth-century contactees, which in this case can be traced back to the life and teachings of Helena Petovna Blavatsky (1831–91), whose Theosophical ideas are clearly paralleled in the claims of many contactees. Blavatsky, a Russian immigrant to the United States, drew heavily upon the teachings of eastern philosophy as well as upon the ideas propounded by the nineteenth-century spiritualist movement to produce a form of spiritualism with a more developed and systematic doctrinal philosophy than was usual for spiritualism.

In 1877, Blavatsky released *Isis Unveiled*, a book that leveled an attack against both traditional Christianity and mainstream science and defended the truth of Blavatsky's own version of occultism. Ten years later *The Secret Doctrine* articulated Blavatsky's views concerning the history of the universe and the history of humanity. In these books and others, Blavatsky made several claims that would come to be important for the twentieth-century contactee movement. First, Blavatsky offered a version of pantheism in which god is present throughout the universe and in which human consciousness shares in the greater universal consciousness. Second, human consciousness shares in the eternity of the universe through reincarnation, which proceeds in a positive direction, that is, humans are able to move forward in the progressive development of human nature. According to Theosophy, human history shows the evolution of human nature from the pure spirit of humanity's beginnings through the ages of Hyperborea, Lemuria, and Atlantis, to the present stage, which is characterized by the awakening of humanity's spiritual nature through the teachings of Theosophy.

This belief in the cultural and spiritual evolution of humanity provides a third important connection with the contactee movement, the idea that the real history of humanity is markedly different from that found in mainstream theories of humanity's past. Theosophy provides a forgotten history of past civilizations, such as Atlantis, that surpassed our own in many ways. Fourth, humans who have already reached elevated states of spiritual awareness may communicate and offer assistance to those struggling upon a lesser plane of existence. These guides are known as Mahatmas or Ascended Masters. Blavatsky and her followers claimed that much of their knowledge had been granted through contact with just such figures.

Two of the most important of these Ascended Masters are Koot Hoomi and Morya. Blavatsky claimed to have had contact with these representatives of the Adept Brotherhood, a group of advanced beings engaged in assisting the human race in the transition to spiritual awareness. It was from their teachings that Blavatsky was able to acquire knowledge of the occult truths. In addition, Blavatsky claimed to have placed these masters in touch with her friend, A. P. Sinnet, who received frequent letters from Koot Hoomi and Morya. For most Theosophists the writings of Blavatsky and the letters of the Ascended Masters as recorded by Sinnet form the foundation of their doctrine.

Blavatsky wrote of her contacts:

> When, years ago, we first travelled over the East, exploring the penetralia of its deserted sanctuaries, two saddening and ever-recurring questions oppressed our thoughts: *Where*, WHO, WHAT *is* GOD? *Who ever saw the* IMMORTAL SPIRIT *of man, so as to be able to assure himself of man's immortality?* . . . It was while most anxious to solve these perplexing problems that we came into contact with certain men, endowed with such mysterious powers and such profound knowledge that we may truly designate them as the sages of the Orient. To their instructions we lent a ready ear.

According to Blavatsky, the knowledge imparted by the Masters was an ancient wisdom preserved from the glory days of humanity by the secret society. She wrote,

> From the first ages of man, the fundamental truths of all that we are permitted to know on earth was in the safe keeping of the adepts of the sanctuary. Those guardians of the primitive divine revelation, who had solved every problem that is within the grasp of human intellect, were bound together by a universal freemasonry of science and philosophy, which formed one unbroken chain around the globe. (Helena Blavatsky, *Isis Unveiled*, online edition, Pasadena, CA, Theosophical University Press, vol I: vi and 37–8, at http://www.theosociety.org/pasadena/isis/iu1-00in.htm)

This does not mean, however, that Blavatsky had received all of the material while in the physical presence of the Masters. Rather, much of her communication with the teachers occurred over a great distance through thought transference.

Every word of [esoteric] information found in my writings comes from the teachings of our Eastern Masters; and many a passage in these works has been written by me under their dictation. In saying this no supernatural claim is urged, for no miracle is performed by such a dictation. Space and distance do not exist for thought; and if two persons are in perfect mutual psycho-magnetic rapport, and of these two, one is a great Adept in Occult Sciences, then thought-transference and dictation of whole pages, become as easy and as comprehensible at the distance of ten thousand miles as the transference of two words across a room. (Helena Blavatsky, *From Long Sealed Ancient Fountains*, online edition, Blavatsky Study Center, 2000, http://www.blavatskyarchives.com/theosophy1.htm)

Blavatsky's Theosophy was a mingling of eastern philosophy with western spiritualism, especially with spiritualism's emphasis upon channeling as a form of communication with spirits or elevated beings. While traditional spiritualism had channeled the spirits of the dead, Theosophy channeled the teachings of great masters alive in the Far East. While spiritualism offered only the most limited of teachings to accompany its showy séances, relying on showmanship and emotion to attract and hold the attention of interested parties, Theosophy drew upon eastern philosophy for its message, a message at the core of its appeal. These elements, eastern philosophy and the channeling of higher beings, found a hospitable climate in the flying saucer craze of the mid-twentieth century. Before we get there, however, there is one more historical antecedent that warrants our attention.

— The Shaver Mystery —

Most UFO chronologies treat the years between the late nineteenth century's airship mystery and the sightings by Kenneth Arnold of flying saucers as a period of quiet in the unfolding UFO story. When the years before Kenneth Arnold's sighting are discussed, it is usually only in reference to 'foo fighters,' those strange, quickly moving lights seen by aircraft pilots during World War II. However, there was much more interest in extraterrestrials and their spacecraft during this period than is normally acknowledged. Of particular importance was what came to be called the 'Shaver Mystery.'

UFO religion

The Shaver Mystery unfolded in the pages of the pulp science-fiction magazine *Amazing Stories*. The mystery began when Ray Palmer, editor of the magazine, received a rather eccentric letter from Richard Sharpe Shaver of Pennsylvania. Legend has it that one of Palmer's staff read the letter and tossed it into the trash. To make a point – though what point I am not quite sure – Palmer retrieved the letter from the wastebasket and published it in the next issue of the magazine. The response from readers was overwhelming. As Palmer gave more and more attention to Shaver's story, freely rewriting and embellishing his work as he saw fit, circulation for *Amazing Stories* continued to grow.

Shaver's story was, to say the least, extremely odd. He told of how he began to hear strange voices while welding on the Ford assembly line in 1932. Some years later he encountered a blind girl named Nydia, who led him to an underground tunnel complex. There Shaver encountered the subterranean residents, robots called deros and teros. The deros and teros were descendants of an extraterrestrial race that had inhabited the earth in the distant past, the Titan-Atlans, residents while on earth of the now lost continent of Atlantis. Dangerous radiation from the sun had sent the Titan-Atlans underground. Later, as the radiation levels continued to grow, the Titan-Atlans were forced to evacuate the planet altogether, leaving behind their robots. The teros maintain the positive energy of their creators while the deros' energy has deteriorated because of their exposure to the sun's radiation. These two races fight an eons-long battle of good versus evil. We humans are descendants of robot races from space, our fates controlled by the clashes and conflicts between the deros and the teros.

When Shaver first contacted Palmer he shared with him an ancient alphabet. Each letter of the alphabet, which corresponded with each letter of the modern English alphabet, was symbolic of an important concept. Words, therefore, could be analyzed into their component meanings by determining the meaning of each letter in each word. The Shaver alphabet consisted of the English alphabet annotated with each letter's appropriate meaning.

The Shaver/Palmer stories began with 'I Remember Lemuria' in March 1945. This article is a first-person account of the exodus from the earth by the Titan-Atlans, told by Mion, a member of one of the lesser, and thus abandoned, races. All four issues of *Amazing Stories* for 1945 contained a Shaver story, each a little weirder than the previous ones. The deros were described as kidnapping surface dwellers and devouring them. They used mind-control devices to shape the course of human history. Readers wrote in with their own stories of encounters with the evil underworld robots. Strange aerial sightings were reported, circular craft identified as belonging to the subterranean races or to their, and our, spacefaring ancestors.

Then in 1947, when Kenneth Arnold reported seeing flying discs over Washington State, all the world was suddenly interested in the phenomenon. Palmer soon left *Amazing Stories* and started his own magazine, *Fate,* which had as its premier article 'I Did See the Flying Disks' by none other than Kenneth Arnold himself. As interest in Shaver declined, interest in Arnold rose.

Arnold would prove to be not only bigger than Shaver, but bigger than Palmer as well. The flying saucer wave kicked off by the 1947 sighting would move beyond Palmer's pulp magazine environment. Donald Keyhoe and others would begin to investigate saucer sightings in earnest but with disdain for the Palmer/Shaver mythology. There would be no room for tales of good versus evil in the accounts of Moore and Hynek. The mythology would live on, however, altered here and there and freely mixed with Theosophy and the pulp science fiction of Palmer's *Amazing Stories* with the shared mythology of Atlantis and Lemuria cropping up from time to time.

In those early days the proponents of a more spiritual approach to UFOs were often seen as opponents to Keyhoe and the proponents of 'nuts and bolts' ufology. They were thought of as the 'lunatic fringe.' It would be a mistake to say that they were the fringe, however, as their numbers were quite large. It is probably also a mistake to call them 'lunatics' unless one takes that word back to its ancient association with the moon. Indeed, they were very interested in the moon: the alien settlements on its dark side, the planet Clarion hidden behind its gentle glow, its reminder that the earth is not alone in a universe of pinpoint lights but accompanied by other earths, each with the potential to contain other civilizations,

civilizations with answers to our problems and the willingness to lend a helping hand.

— George Adamski —

George Adamski was the embodiment of the collaboration between Theosophy and pulp science fiction. Rooted in the Theosophist tradition, Adamski founded the 'Royal Order of Tibet' in Southern California in 1934. There he taught Theosophist ideas under the title of 'universal laws' or 'universal progressive Christianity.' Until his contact experience in 1952, Adamski dropped in and out of Theosophist circles, playing the part of the 'Professor,' though never holding any sort of graduate degree. He was the author of several books and pamphlets prior to his extraterrestrial experiences; *Wisdom Master of the Far East* was published in 1936, followed by such works as *Telepathy: The Cosmic or Universal Language* and *The Science of Life Study Course*. The sort of simple message propounded by Adamski is shown in an excerpt from a 1937 publication entitled *The Kingdom of Heaven on Earth*:

> The little sunbeam was traveling through space and on her journey she contacted one who told her of a dreadful thing called darkness. 'Why, I have never seen darkness and I have traveled far,' said the sunbeam. 'But I will go still farther until I have found this thing that makes men tremble and fear for it interests me.' So the sunbeam sought in every corner of the earth; she went to the lowest planes of life and she went to the highest planes of life but everywhere she went she found only light and loveliness and things were beautiful. At last she returned to the one who had told her of the darkness. 'Surely,' she said, 'you are mistaken about the thing called darkness for I have traveled the whole world over, I have sought in every crevice and corner of the earth but I have found only light.'
>
> And so should it be with every ray that emanates from the Father's throne. 'Let there be light,' God said, and there was light. And there is light that abides within each living thing. (George Adamski Foundation International, at http://www.gafintl-adamski.com/html/heaven.htm)

In 1944, along with a group of followers, Adamski moved to a ranch at the foot of Mount Palomar. In 1949 they moved up the mountain and began to operate a small roadside restaurant. The restaurant's customers were mostly tourists on their way to and from the famous Mount Palomar Observatory. His proximity to the observatory would be fortuitous for Adamski as many would associate his Mount Palomar address with the observatory and assume that he was affiliated with the famous telescope. He wasn't.

During the late 1940s Adamski began to turn his attention to extraterrestrial subjects. As early as 1946 he speculated concerning life on other planets. His ideas concerning extraterrestrial entities were clearly influenced by his Theosophical background. He wrote then in *Life on Other Planets:*

> There is no longer a question as to whether there are other inhabited planets in the universe but as to the type of beings who live there. And as science has through mathematical and scientific calculation proven the habitability of other planets, they shall by the same method analyze the character of the intelligence upon them. There are very few people today who do not believe in a continuance of life. A few there are who believe that death of the body is the end of all and there are a great number who are satisfied with a mythical heaven and hell where the soul either dwells forever in Celestial bliss or gradually simmers away in a flaming pit of fire. There are others who believe in an eternal nirvana where man is lost to all manifestation and active expression. But how much more logical and in keeping with a divine intelligence would it be to assume that eternal life expresses itself in evolving stages of progress from one planet to another throughout that universe whose boundaries have no limit. How simple for the soul of man to go on, finding rebirth in suitable form on each planet as his wisdom expands and permits further evolvement. Perhaps the early Druids had some hint of this truth within their being when they looked to the Moon as the Paradise for souls who had earned immortality. (George Adamski Foundation International, at http://www.gafintl-adamski.com/html/GAArt.htm)

Though there is little in Adamski's speculations concerning life on other planets and human reincarnation to higher planes that had not been articulated by earlier Theosophists, Adamski was to rise to prominence because he was able to connect his Theosophical speculations with the UFO craze that erupted in 1947. In 1949 he published a science-fiction novel called *Pioneers of Space: A Trip to the*

UFO religion

Moon, Mars, and Venus, telling a story of contact with beings from other planets in our solar system. Adamski's fictional extraterrestrials were humanoid and traveled in cigar-shaped craft; natives of the moon, Mars, and Venus, the 'pioneers of space' were quite civilized and fond of banquets and polite conversation. These ideas, presented as fiction in 1949, would soon be presented as fact.

According to Desmond Leslie and Adamski's best-selling book, *Flying Saucers Have Landed* (1955) sightings of spacecraft from his home at Mount Palomar culminated in actual contact with an extraterrestrial on November 20, 1952. Adamski, along with a group of friends that included George Hunt Williamson, observed a cigar-shaped object hovering in the air near Desert Center, California. After witnessing the landing of a small craft nearby, Adamski left his friends behind and went towards the area of the landing. Soon he was approached by a figure who was walking across the desert as if to meet him. Adamski wrote:

> As I approached him a strange feeling came upon me and I became cautious. At the same time I looked round to reassure myself that we were both in full sight of my companions. Outwardly there was no reason for this feeling, for the man looked like any other man, and I could see he was somewhat smaller than I and considerably younger. There were only two outstanding differences that I noticed as I neared him.
>
> His trousers were not like mine. They were in style much like ski trousers and with a passing thought I wondered why he wore such out here on the desert.
>
> His hair was long, reaching to his shoulder, and was blowing in the wind as was mine. But this was not too strange for I have seen a number of men who wore their hair almost that long. . . .
>
> Suddenly, as though a veil was removed from my mind, the feeling of caution left me so completely that I was no longer aware of my friends or whether they were observing me as they had been told to do. By this time we were quite close. He took four steps toward me, bringing us within arm's length of each other.
>
> Now, for the first time I fully realised that I was in the presence of a man from space – A HUMAN BEING FROM ANOTHER WORLD!

The description continues:

He was about five feet, six inches in height and weighed – according to our standards – about 135 pounds. And I would estimate him to be about 28 years of age, although he could have been much older.

He was round faced with an extremely high forehead; large, but calm, grey-green eyes, slightly aslant at the outer corners; with slightly higher cheek bones than an Occidental, but not so high as an Indian or an Oriental; a finely chiseled nose, not conspicuously large; and an average size mouth with beautiful white teeth that shone when he smiled or spoke.

As nearly as I can describe his skin coloring would be an even, medium-colored suntan. And it did not look to me as though he had ever had to shave, for there was no more hair on his face than on a child's.

His hair was sandy in colour and hung in beautiful waves to his shoulders, glistening more beautifully than any woman's I have ever seen. (Leslie and Adamski, 1953: 194 and 195)

Conversation with the beautiful spaceman revealed that his name was Orthon and that he was from the planet Venus, though in an earlier life he had lived upon earth. He also revealed that space visitors were behind many of the flying discs seen around the world, that sometimes their craft did crash, and that many visitors from other planets lived on earth unbeknownst to terrestrial humans. After the Venusian had returned to his craft Adamski discovered clearly defined footprints in the sand, distinguished by strange symbols and figures. George Hunt Williamson made casts of the prints, a sketch of which is included in the book. Adamski's book also included pictures taken through his telescope, showing both cigar-shaped 'mother ships' and disc-shaped 'scout ships.' These photographs, especially of the scout ships, would become iconic images of the early saucer wave.

In Adamski's sequel, *Inside the Space Ships*, he told of other encounters with beings from space, including Venusians, Martians, and Saturnians. He also described his ride in the extraterrestrial craft. Taken to the moon, he was allowed to see the many secrets of the 'dark side,' including cities, landing strips, and snow. Most significantly, it was while he was aboard the spaceships that Adamski encountered Ascended Masters and teachers reminiscent of those in Theosophy. One teacher shared with Adamski information that had already been a part of his earlier teachings, namely the idea that reincarnation is a process that moves the spirit upward on an interplanetary journey. According to the great teacher:

> The first fact your people must realize is that the inhabitants of other worlds are not fundamentally different from Earth men. The purpose of life on other worlds is basically the same as yours. Inherent in all mankind, however deeply buried it may be, is the yearning to rise to something higher. Your school system on Earth is, in a sense, patterned after the universal progress of life. For in your schools you progress from grade to grade and from school to school, toward a higher and fuller education. In the same way, man progresses from planet to planet, and from system to system toward an ever higher understanding and evolvement in universal growth and service. (Adamski, 1955: 88–9)

The teacher went on to explain to Adamski that the growing frequency of their visits to earth and their contacts with individuals such as Adamski were driven by their concerns with the development of nuclear weapons. Though the radiation from the bombs had not yet left the earth's atmosphere, it was of concern to the 'Space Brothers' because it would soon prove deadly to earth's population. Their worries extended beyond their concerns for the inhabitants of earth, however. They also feared for the very galaxy itself.

> If, however, mankind on Earth should release such power against one another in full warfare, a large part of Earth's population could be annihilated, your soil rendered sterile, your waters poisoned and barren to life for many years to come. It is possible that the body of your planet itself could be mutilated to an extent that would destroy balance in our galaxy.

Their visits to earth are meant to assist the citizens of the planet to develop beyond their current stage of prejudice and violence into a true appreciation of the universal brotherhood and the divine nature of all life.

> We see the Divine Consciousness expressing Itself through the growth of any and all forms, from the smallest to the largest. We have learned that nothing, no form, whatever, can be what it is without life passing through it, or supporting it. And the life we

recognize is the Divine Supreme Intelligence. (Adamski, 1955: 91–2 and 205–6)

The true message the aliens wish to share is that when one causes harm to another living thing, one is in reality causing harm to oneself.

Not everything in Adamski's encounter was so serious, however. He learned much about the social life of extraterrestrials. For example, they love to have parties and to dance, though they are not fans of all the forms of dance practiced among the residents of the earth. 'We could derive no joy from the kick, wiggle, and hop we have observed on your Earth, during which a man and a woman clutch each other ferociously one moment and fling each other off the next' (Adamski, 1955: 107).

Adamski's stories of contact with extraterrestrials, and his photographs of their spacecraft, were warmly received by many in the Theosophical tradition and by many who were enamored of the flying saucer phenomena. On the other hand, he was also vilified by those in the UFO community who wanted to maintain the distinction between the phenomena and any sort of religious claims. Opinion on Adamski was sharply divided. Some thought him sincere and believed his accounts; others argued that he was little more than a charlatan; still others accused him of being mentally ill. Love him or hate him, Adamski was the original contactee, the first person to seize the imagination of popular culture with tales of actual meetings with spacemen and actual rides on spacecraft. Clearly, all of the other contacts and contactees would flow through Adamski and his blend of Blavatsky and Shaver, Theosophy and science fiction, some closer to one, some closer to the other, almost all of them confident and optimistic, like Adamski himself, that the visitors in the flying discs sought only good.

> Let us be friendly. Let us recognize and welcome the men from other worlds! THEY ARE HERE AMONG US. Let us be wise enough to learn from those who can teach us much – who will be our friends if we but let them. (Leslie and Adamski, 1953: 222)

— Truman Bethurum —

Following closely on the heels of Adamski's revelations, Truman Bethurum began publishing accounts of his contacts with alien visitors in magazines and newspapers in 1953. Bethurum, a mechanic on a crew engaged in road construction in the California desert, published his account as the book *Aboard a Flying Saucer* in 1954. In this book he recounts multiple contacts with the crew of the flying saucer named 'The Admiral's Scow.' The Scow and her crew were from the planet Clarion, a planet hidden from detection from the earth because it lies on the other side of the moon. His first encounter occurred while he was sleeping in his truck late one night. He awakened to discover his vehicle was surrounded by eight or ten diminutive men, each standing between four and five feet tall. Bethurum, like Adamski, seemed to have an eye for fashion and gave a detailed description of the beings' attire.

> Suddenly I realized that there was something different about these little men; not that they were dwarfs. They were fully developed small men. The real difference which struck me so forcibly was that they all seemed to be wearing some sort of uniform – unfamiliar to me. All but two or three of them wore black billed caps with a black band around the bottom. Of the bareheaded ones, all whose hair was black and crew cut, one's hair was wavy. And all of them wore jackets like cowboys and trousers of material which reflected a blue-grayish cast under the bright moonlight. Their dark olive hued faces were bland and without lines or blemishes, like the skin was taut and hard over the bone structure. (Bethurum, 1954: 35)

Climbing down from his truck, Bethurum was suprised by the sight of an enormous saucer-shaped craft. Apparently made of burnished steel, the craft was 300 feet in diameter and six yards deep at the center. It was hovering a few feet above the ground.

Even more startling to Bethurum than the crew of little men or the silently hovering saucer was the captain of the vessel, Aura Rhanes. Getting over the initial shock of seeing a female commander, Bethurum was soon entranced by her beauty and personality:

> She was a trifle shorter than any of the men I had seen. Her smooth skin was a beautiful olive and roses, and her brown-eyed

flashing smile seemed to make her complexion appear more glowing. I am sure she wore no makeup, but she certainly needed none.

So this queen of women was the lady captain!

She wore no jewelry, not even a buckle on her belt.

Her black hair was short and brushed into an upward curl at the ends, and she wore jauntily tilted on one side of her proudly held head a black and red beret. She was standing before a great wide flat topped desk, with her graceful hands resting upon it. Her bodice was of some fitted material which looked like black velvet, with sort sleeves decorated with a small red ribbon bow. The top of her skirt, which I could see above the edge of the desk, was the most radiant red material I have ever seen. It looked like wool and we set all around in small flat pleats. (Bethurum, 1954: 40–1)

The planet Clarion was described as a near-perfect Eden. Bethurum learned that there are no traffic jams and that all roadways were wide, smooth, and level. Transportation is quick and easy in 'little neutornic jeeps.' Accidents are avoided by anti-magnetic flashes that kept the vehicles from making contact with each other. The people of Clarion worship a supreme deity, who is omniscient, omnipresent, and omnipotent. Like Adamski's Venusians, the Clarions like to dance. Aura Rhames told Bethurum that their planet had many styles of dancing: polkas, square dances, old time dances, folk dances, and ballets.

According to Bethurum's own account his second wife divorced him because she was jealous of Captain Aura Rhanes, perhaps with good reason. Columba Krebs, an artist who worked closely with Bethurum, reported that he had hired a secretary whom he claimed looked remarkably liked the tiny captain. In any event, Bethurum seems to have moved on, marrying his third wife at one of Van Tassel's Giant Rock saucer conventions

— Orfeo Angelucci —

According to his book, *The Secret of the Saucers* (1955), Orfeo Angelucci began to experience contacts with extraterrestrials in the summer of 1952. This book, edited by Ray Palmer, tells the stories of those contacts beginning with a strange experience that overcame Angelucci while driving his car in Los Angeles. (In LA, not that unusual, I would think.) Seemingly led by internal forces to a particular location, Angelucci was told to get out of his car. As he did so he saw two pulsating lights hovering in front of him. Suddenly feeling very thirsty, Angelucci heard a voice say 'Drink from the crystal cup you will find on the fender of your car, Orfeo' (Angelucci, 1955: 6).

> Astonished at his words, I glanced down and saw a kind of goblet on the car fender. It glistened in the soft light. Hesitantly I lifted it to my lips and tasted the drink. It was the most delicious beverage I had ever tasted. I drained the cup. Even as I was drinking a feeling of strength and well being swept over me and all of my unpleasant symptoms vanished. (Angelucci, 1955: 7)

In a later encounter, Angelucci was taken aboard an igloo-shaped craft. Finding himself within a circular, domed room Angelucci noted that the walls were made of an ethereal, iridescent substance that seemed to give off light; the room was completely quiet. Directly in front of him was a reclining chair. Beginning to panic, Angelucci was soon calmed by very familiar music and recognized the melody of his favorite song, 'Fools Rush In.' According to Angelucci, the sounds of the music took away all of his fear, he realized he was safe with those who bothered to know about his favorite song, 'So open up your heart and let this fool rush in . . .'.

Taken into orbit to view the earth, Angelucci was told to weep for the planet, as the Hebrew prophets were told to weep for Jerusalem.

> The voice said softly: 'Weep, Orfeo. Let tears unblind your eyes. For at this moment we weep with you for Earth and her Children. For all of its apparent beauty Earth is a purgatorial world among the planets evolving intelligent life. Hate, selfishness and cruelty rise from many parts of it like a dark mist.' (Angelucci, 1955: 24)

To Angelucci it was revealed that the earth is a battleground between the forces of good and the forces of evil. It was also revealed that this has not always been the case. In the distant past another planet had circled the sun as a member of this solar system. This planet was originally the home of the race that now inhabits the earth. On that planet they never knew pain, sorrow, or death. Unfortunately, their great and advanced state of being made them proud and arrogant; they fought great wars among themselves and turned against the 'Great Giver of Life.' Finally, they destroyed their home world, the remains of which constitute the asteroid belt between Mars and Jupiter. In order to restore balance to the cosmos, those beings were reborn upon the earth, forced to struggle once again with pain and sorrow as a means of achieving their redemption. Eventually, through the cycle of rebirth, all of the residents of earth will achieve redemption.

Visitors from other planets are coming to earth now, as they have for centuries, to tilt the balance in favor of the forces of light. Jesus himself is perhaps the greatest example of the extraterrestrial mission to earth, as the voice reveals to Angelucci.

> In allegorical language Christ is indeed the Son of God. The star that burned over Bethlehem is a cosmic fact. It announced the birth on your planet of an entity not of Earth's evolution. He is Lord of the Flame – an infinite entity of the sun. Out of compassion for mankind's suffering He became flesh and blood and entered the hell of ignorance, woe and evil. As the Sun Spirit who sacrificed himself for the children of woe he has become a part of the oversoul of mankind and the world spirit. He differs from all other world teachers. (Angelucci, 1955: 33)

The climactic moment in Angelucci's experience soon followed, as the strains of the Lord's Prayer were played 'as though by thousands of violins.' With tears pouring from his eyes, Angelucci was filled with humility and gratitude for the work done by his celestial contacts. As a culmination to the epiphany,

> Above the exquisite strains of the melody, the voice said: 'Beloved friend of Earth, we baptize you now in the true light of the worlds eternal.'
> A blinding white beam flashed from the dome of the craft. Momentarily I seemed partially to lose consciousness. Everything expanded into a great shimmering white light. I seemed to be projected beyond Time and Space and was conscious only of light, Light, LIGHT! Orfeo, Earth, the past were as nothing, a dark dream of a moment. And that dream unfolded before my eyes in a swift panorama. Every event of my life upon Earth was crystal clear to me – *and then memory of all my previous lives upon Earth returned.* IN THAT SUBLIME MOMENT I KNEW THE

> MYSTERY OF LIFE! Also, I realized with a terrible certainty that we are all – each one of us – TRAPPED IN ETERNITY and ALLOTTED ONLY ONE BRIEF AWARENESS AT A TIME! (Angelucci, 1955: 34)

With this element, this baptism into the true light of worlds eternal, Orfeo Angelucci brought his contact experience full circle, back to that moment when he had taken the chalice of communion from the fender of his car. Through these new sacraments, or should we say these celestial versions of ancient earth sacraments, Angelucci was made a member of the universal brotherhood.

— Howard Menger —

Unlike other contactees, Howard Menger claimed that his experience with extraterrestrial visitors began when he was only a child. Though he did not tell his story until 1959, under the guidance of Gray Barker, in the book *From Outer Space to You*, Menger claimed to have had contacts from as early as 1932, when he was only ten years old. As an adult, he recalled the first such incident clearly.

> There, sitting on a rock by the brook, was the most exquisite woman my young eyes had ever beheld! The warm sunlight caught the highlights of her long golden hair as it cascaded around her face and shoulders. The curves of her lovely body were delicately contoured – revealed through the translucent material of clothing which reminded me of the habit of skiers.
>
> I halted in my tracks, and for a moment my breath stopped. I was not frightened, but an overwhelming wonderment froze me to the spot.
>
> She turned her head in my direction.
>
> Even though very young, the feeling I received was unmistakable.
>
> It was a tremendous surge of warmth, love, and physical attraction which emanated from her to me.
>
> Suddenly all my anxiety was gone and I approached her as one would an old friend or loved one.
>
> She seemed to radiate and glow as she sat on the rock, and I wondered if it were due to the unusual quality of the material she wore, which had a shimmering, shiny texture not unlike but far surpassing the sheen of nylon. The clothing had no buttons, fas-

teners, or seams I could discern. She wore no makeup, which would have been unnecessary to the fragile transparency of her camellia-like skin with pinkish undertones.

Her eyes, opalescent discs of gold, turned their smiling affection on me with a tranquil luminescence. (Menger, 1959: 21–2)

This would be only the first of many encounters with extraterrestrial visitors. Fourteen years later, he even met his original contact again and was amazed that she had not aged at all, though he discovered that his own interests in her had changed remarkably from the age of ten to the age of twenty-four.

Menger was enlisted to assist the visitors in their attempt to establish themselves undercover upon the earth. Through telepathic messages he was instructed to meet his friends at designated field locations. Once there he was instructed to do things that would be quite simple for him, but which would have been very difficult for the aliens. Though in appearance they resembled the residents of earth – except for the long hair of the men – their acclimatization to the earth's climate and customs was not yet complete. At least on one occasion he discovered just how different the alien culture was.

Such tasks were not without their moments of humor, and I think the visitors enjoyed them as much as I did. I remember one time when I was asked to purchase several complete outfits of female clothing. Feeling it would be embarrassing and somewhat difficult to explain why I was buying so many outfits, I purchased them in separate shops.

I bought what I thought was the appropriate sizes and showed up at the point of contact. The women went into the next room from which I soon heard a series of giggles and groans. Finally the door opened and the bras were flung out. They apologized, saying they just could not wear them, and they never had. Just why I don't know, and you may be certain that I felt it wise not to ask! (Menger, 1959: 65)

Menger provides information about the visitors in a series of questions and answers. For example:

Q. Why do they come here – what is their purpose?
A. To try to awaken within us a yearning for higher understanding so we can help ourselves in preventing any further destruction of our planet, which could conceivably

have a bad effect in our solar system. It is about time we grew up as a humanity. (Menger, 1959: 156)

Do space people already live among us? Yes, they are here in their thousands. Some have come to earth in spacecraft and some have come through the process of rebirth. They could be anyone: your neighbor, the waitress at the restaurant, your co-worker. Their common trait is their love for humanity. Do they believe in God? Yes. They believe in service to the Infinite Father and seek to attain knowledge so that their service to the creator may grow. Jesus was himself a space brother at the highest point of development. Indeed, one of the most important tasks of the space people is to assist earth's inhabitants in the development of their understanding of God.

We [have] noticed and recorded your distorted concepts of what God is with great sorrow and concern for your ignorance. On our view screens thought patterns of God took on many forms and shapes, but most were men, some with beards, some tall, some short, and of course some were stone or wood or metallic idols. Son, we have not seen the Supreme Intelligence in the sense that it is a particular form or shape. God is not a man. To call God a man is to limit that God. God is all. (Menger, 1959: 170)

In addition to their religious mission, however, they also brought to earth a far more practical message. To extend human life and end much human suffering and misery, the residents of earth must change their diet. According to Menger our methods of food production and consumption are perhaps our greatest threat: 'These are the poisons of our world: over consumption of animal proteins, candies, cakes, pastries, white flour, white sugar, alcohol, tobacco, drugs, carbonated drinks, ice cream, and all foods treated by poison sprays, poison gases, commercial fertilizers, bleach, etc' (Menger, 1959: 191).

Also, sodium fluoride added to our water supply distorts our powers of reasoning. The fluoride additive, while good in small doses for our teeth, has a detrimental effect upon our power of will. The fluoride drugs an area of the brain that makes humans more docile. The effects are similar, we are told, to the effects of a prefrontal lobotomy. The fluoride additive, therefore, will render the population submissive and easily controllable by the forces of government and capitalism. A fluoridated individual, exposed to nonstop messages via television, will soon become a slave to merchandisers and governments. You know, I think Menger was on to something.

— Daniel Fry —

According to Daniel Fry's 1954 book *The White Sands Incident* his first encounter with an extraterrestrial took place on July 4, 1949 at the White Sands Proving Ground in New Mexico while he was out for a night time stroll down a seldom-used road. Fry tells the story by quoting from his diary entry from the night of the sighting.

> Tonight I joined the ranks of the F. S. B. (Flying Saucer Believers). Not only have I seen one, I have touched it, entered it, and ridden in it. Also, if I can still trust my senses, I have communicated at some length with the operators.
>
> Now that it has gone, and I am back in my quarters, it seems more and more incredible that it could really have happened. With all the scientific brain and talent that is available at White Sands Proving Grounds, why should I, a simple technician, be chosen, either by chance or design, to be the first human of the present day earth, to ride in a true space vehicle? The improbability of the event is so great that I have almost begun to doubt my own sanity. Naturally, if I were to attempt to convince anyone else that I rode in a 'saucer' tonight, I would soon find myself occupying a nicely padded cell in the nearest Booby Hatch. Still this is the greatest event in my life, and I can't keep it entirely to myself, so I am writing this down exactly as it happened while it is still sharp and clear in my memory.

Fry reports that after being intrigued by a series of strange lights he soon came into contact with what could only be an extraterrestrial craft.

> [H]ere was a craft so far advanced over anything I had ever heard of, that I felt like the backwoods farmer who, on first seeing a giraffe, said, 'Well I see it, but I don't believe it.' My first conscious thought was, 'if the Russians have ships like this, God help America!' But with the thought came the realization that this

could not be a craft from Russia, or anywhere else on earth for that matter; for whoever had built this craft had solved a lot of problems of which our best physicists are only beginning to dream.

Being familiar with aircraft, Fry approached the craft and put out his hand to touch it with his finger. This gesture got quite a reaction from the craft.

> Then a crisp voice came out of the air at my side, 'Better not touch the hull, pal, it's still hot!'
> I had not realized how much tension I was under until the voice suddenly shattered the silence. I leaped backwards several feet, catching my heel in a low bush and sprawling at full length in the sand. I heard something that sounded like a low chuckle and then the voice came again in a somewhat friendlier tone, 'Take it easy, pal, you're among friends.'
> The humiliation of my ungraceful posture, combined with the mild tone of the voice and its familiar phrases, served to sweep away all the fear which I had felt and replaced it with a mild irritation. I arose brushing off my clothes and tugging at a sand burr which had found a home in my hair.
> 'You could have turned the volume down,' I grumbled. 'You didn't have to blast out at me like that. You scared me out of a week's growth.'
> 'Blast out?' the voice hesitated. 'Oh yes, you mean the amplitude of the warning was too great. Sorry, buddy, but you were about to kill yourself and there wasn't time to diddle with controls.' (Fry, 1992: 15, 19 and 22–3)

It was revealed to Fry that the craft was without a crew but was only a remote-controlled cargo ship. Nevertheless, Fry was invited to climb aboard and take a ride, and quite a ride it was. Fry was taken from New Mexico to New York and back in under thirty minutes, traveling at 8,000 miles and hour! Fry, stunned by the view of New York from the spacecraft, wrote,

> If I were a writer or a poet I could, perhaps, do some small justice to the sight which met my eyes as the greatest metropolis in the world rotated slowly before me. Since I am neither a writer nor a poet, but only a simple technician with a limited vocabulary and faltering construction, I fear that it is almost hopeless to make the attempt. At the twenty mile level the lights were much brighter and had greater individuality than they had seemed to have from

the higher level. This was no glowing bed of coals with a few brighter sparks. This was a vast array of millions of blue white diamonds, scintillating and coruscating against a black velvet background. The differing temperatures of the various air strata beneath me, combined with the rapid motion of the ship, caused the lights to twinkle violently, so that the entire city was a sea of pulsing, shimmering luminescence. (Fry, 1992: 52)

In conversations with his extraterrestrial contact, a being called 'Alan,' Fry learned some very important facts about the visitors and about the history of our own planet. In ages past their race had built a great civilization on the continent known to legend as Mu or Lemuria. At the same time in history another great civilization had thrived and been in competition with Lemuria; this was the fabled civilization of Atlantis. The technology of the two civilizations finally reached a point at which the destruction of each civilization by the other was inevitable. A small proportion of the inhabitants fled the destruction by escaping into space. Their descendants are now attempting to make contact with the current residents of the planet in order to help them avoid the kind of destruction that destroyed Lemuria and Atlantis.

Fry followed up his publication of *The White Sands Incident* with the founding of an organization which he called 'Understanding.' The purpose of the group and its eponymous newsletter was to spread information about contact with extraterrestrials as well as Alan's warning about the possible destruction of civilization as we know it. Fry's group was never very large and probably reached its zenith in the mid-1970s when the group received a gift of several acres of land, including eight buildings, which had been designed as the campus of a religious college. The unique buildings were round and remarkably reminiscent of flying saucers. Fry was a regular attendee of the Giant Rock saucer conventions hosted by his friend George Van Tassel.

— George Hunt Williamson —

George Hunt Williamson was a follower of George Adamski, having been in attendance at Adamski's first contact with an extraterrestrial visitor. Williamson's experience with extraterrestrial contacts preceded his relationship with Adamski, however. His history of involvement with Theosophy included participation in William Dudley Pelley's group that emphasized contact with Ascended Masters through automatic writing. Combining this Theosophical background with his own intense interest in the flying saucer phenomenon then sweeping the country, Williamson proceeded to attempt contact with extraterrestrials through the use of a Ouija board. Hearing of Adamski's claims of similar contacts, he was attracted to the older Theosophist and his supporters at Palomar Gardens.

After Adamski began to receive attention from the press and to attract a larger group of followers, Williamson broke with the Palomar group. Continuing to receive his own Ouija board messages from extraterrestrials, he could claim to have as much authority as Adamski himself. Alas, when two contactees have incompatible messages, a break-up is sure to follow. Williamson went on to publish claims concerning his radio contact with extraterrestrials, including Actar of Mercury, Agfa Affa of Uranus, Noro of the Saucer Fleet, and countless others. Most of these radio messages were received in international Morse code. To Williamson it was revealed that not all aliens are friendly. Indeed a fleet of alien craft from Orion is on its way to the planet with evil intents and purposes. The friendly space brothers, however, will surely be able to give us aid as they have throughout history, from the distant past when they revealed to us the first rudiments of civilizations and were mistaken by us for gods, to the present when they come in flying saucers to help us through the crisis of the cold war.

— Frank Stranges —

In December of 1959, according to his book *Stranger at the Pentagon*, The Reverend Frank Stranges was invited to meet a man from another world. While in Washington for an evangelical crusade, Stranges was approached by a friend who worked at the Pentagon and asked Stranges if he would like to make the acquaintance of an individual from another planet who was the top-secret guest of the

US government. Realizing what a rare honor this was, Stranges readily agreed. His friend made the arrangements and soon Stranges found himself on the way to the Pentagon. Passing through Pentagon security as arranged by his friend, he was ushered to a room and told to begin his interview. In the room Stranges found three enlisted men engaged in paperwork at three desks. In the back of the room was another man, not sitting like the others, but standing. Stranges realized this was the man he had come to see.

In shaking the man's hand, Stranges could not help but notice that though his grip was strong his skin was soft like a baby's. His eyes were brown, as was his hair; his complexion was ordinary, appearing as if he had a slight tan. Shockingly, however, Stranges discovered that the man had no fingerprints! This was to be but the first of many confirmations of the man's extraterrestrial origins.

Though the man was wearing normal earth clothing, Stranges learned that the man's personal garment had been given to researchers for analysis. Walking to a nearby closet, the visitor produced a glittering one-piece garment. Stranges writes, 'I asked him of the material from which it was made. He answered, "IT IS MADE OF A MATERIAL NOT OF THIS EARTH."' He went on to explain that the suit had been tested at 'temperatures above that of the melting point of steel' and was not even warmed by the heat. Likewise it had passed the 'acid test.' The acid, Stranges was assured, rolled off the suit 'like water from the back of a duck.' When the investigators tried to pierce the suit with a diamond drill the drill overheated and the diamond snapped. (Frank E. Stranges, 'My Friend from Beyond Earth', pamphlet)

The visitor claimed that he had come to earth in order to help humanity 'return to the Lord.' He had been on earth for three years at the time of his meeting with Stranges, meeting with those who were open to his presence and his message. His home world was revealed to be Venus, where the absence of fingerprints was unremarkable. Fingerprints, Stranges was told, are the mark of a fallen people. He claimed to be one of seventy-seven Venusians currently visiting the earth.

Then, as Stranges turned to leave the room, the visitor spoke to him once more.

> PLEASE KEEP YOUR FAITH AND LEAVE THE SAME WAY
> THAT YOU CAME IN. CONTINUE TO SEEK FIRST THE KING-
> DOM OF GOD AND HIS RIGHTEOUSNESS AND ALL OTHER
> THINGS WILL, IN TIME, BE ADDED UNTO YOU AND
> YOURS. GOODBY FOR NOW, AND GOD BLESS YOU AND
> KEEP YOU ALWAYS. (Stranges, 'My Friend from Beyond
> Earth')

Later, Stranges would reveal the name of his extraterrestrial friend
as 'Valiant Thor' and describe other more detailed encounters and
conversations with the Venusian. He would also circulate a photo-
graph that he claimed to be of 'Val' and two of his Venusian friends.

— Borealis —

Appended to later editions of Daniel Fry's *The White Sands Incident*
is 'An Extraterrestrial Statement' by Rolf Telano. Rolf Telano is a
pseudonym for Ralph Merridette Holland, a science-fiction author
who either did not want his work with fiction to raise any doubts
about the veracity of the extraterrestrial statement or did not want
his claims of alien contact to sully his literary reputation. In any
event, 'An Extraterrestrial Statement' purports to be just that, an
official statement given by a being named Borealis who hailed from
the planet Venus. Borealis revealed that she was a member of the
extraterrestrial race of Nors, a race responsible for the creation of
humans as physical entities in the Garden of Eden, the biological
laboratory of the Elder Races.

> The Nors, who operate most (but not all) of the strange craft seen
> in your skies, are one of the Elder Races or 'Guardians' of your
> planet. At present time we are the largest group operating in this
> solar system, although there are also members of other races
> present. These Elder Races have been guarding your planet ever
> since the first human appeared on it. At the same time they have
> been attempting to tutor you, and to guide your development,
> using subtle pressures which would not hamper your own self
> development. . . .
> These Elder Races created the physical bodies of your ances-
> tors. They did not, of course, create their spiritual bodies, since
> this is beyond the ability of any mortal. Those parts of the 'Self'
> are directly of and from the Unnameable. (Fry, 1992: 15–16)

Borealis told of how the earth was once circled by two great natural satellites, but that the second moon, Azaltan or Bal, had been destroyed. This destruction caused the orbit of Luna to be changed so that it was no longer inhabitable. The Lunarians managed to escape to earth and are known in earth legends as the Atlans of Atlantis. Their civilization and influence spread throughout the Mediterranean world. Because of an increase of radiation on the surface of the earth, the Atlans were forced underground; most of the underworld's inhabitants have now returned to their home worlds. According to Borealis, Shaver's stories are fictionalized accounts of what actually happened.

Borealis revealed that Jesus Christ was the result of a mating between a human woman and a being from another world. This experiment in hybridization was an attempt by the Space Patrol, under the guidance of the Galaxy Council, to share the truth about the Unnameable to the people of earth in the hope that their future might be changed for the better. According to Borealis, the current plan by the Space Patrol and the Galaxy Council is much more subtle. It is 'to simply place individual grains of sand in an attempt to alter humanity's future for the better.' The true mission of Borealis, of the Space Patrol, and of the Galaxy Council is to assist the earth in its growth and development, to lead us to a higher level of maturity, to lead us forward until we too are at home in the stars.

Perhaps most importantly of all, Borealis makes it clear that even though the space brothers and sisters are here to help in our spiritual maturation we should not regard them as gods.

> We are neither demons come to destroy you, nor gods come to magically deliver you. We are, in the final analysis, 'just people' – people who are not greatly different from Earthfolk deep inside – people who live and love, and hope and fear, and, on occasion, laugh and weep. We regard you and greet you as 'Brothers' in the truest sense of the word.' (Fry, 1992: 11)

◆ ◆ ◆

Madame Blavatsky, Richard Shaver, Ray Palmer, George Adamski, Truman Bethurum, Orfeo Angelucci, Howard Menger, Daniel Fry, George Hunt Williamson, Frank Stranges – an odd cast of characters even without the extraterrestrials themselves: Orthon, Actar of Mercury, Agfa Affa from Uranus, Noro of the Saucer Fleet, Valiant Thor, Alan, Aura, and Borealis. And we mustn't forget the stories – stories of footprints in the desert sand with untranslatable messages for humanity, alien dance parties, tiny alien saucer captains wearing cute berets, space sacraments, space women without bras, aliens who use words like 'pal' and 'buddy' and 'diddle,' messages from outer space sent in international Morse code, beings without fingerprints who wear uniforms impervious to acid, the Space Patrol and the Galaxy Council. Okay, this is a little weird, a little funny, a little strange.

I see why the 'nuts and bolts' ufologists didn't like these guys. Adamski and company weren't interested in conducting scientific investigations. They were interested in the meaning of life, the origins of human existence, clear guidance on how we should live our lives, and the chance at redemption from the cares of the world. I also see why the contactees had little patience with the 'nuts and bolts' crew. They were missing the point. Why obsess over lights in the night sky or crash wreckage in the desert when you can communicate with the space beings directly, reach out and touch them, take a ride on their spacecraft? Why focus on nuts and bolts when the very secrets of the universe are readily available to all who would seek? Why spend your time worrying about little gray aliens who go bump in the night when you can have an intergalactic affair with Captain Aura Rhanes or discover the secret of life from a Nors Venusian named Borealis?

The space brothers and sisters offer something different from the shudder of awe one feels in the face of a natural wonder, something different to the mystery of the spaceman's grave in Texas, and they offer it while all decked out in acid-proof ski pants, beautiful long hair, and stylish berets. Short, bug-eyed, gray-skinned creatures or tentacled monstrosities are rarely found in the presence of the contactees because the contactee movement is a celebration of our humanity. It is a cautious celebration because of the lurking danger of The Bomb, but it is a celebration nonetheless. The aliens look like us – they are us, only better looking, more advanced, more spiritual, and more ethical. They are us – or rather they are what we should be, what we will be. (Okay, maybe not the ski pants and beret.)

I like the contactees. Their 'crazy sincerity' is something that I find quite compelling. Even if their message did border on the trite, at least it could do no harm. We are not alone in the universe. All around us are others like us, our big brothers and sisters perhaps, who will both protect us and show us the way. Maybe we'll get to ride in their cool atomic-powered spaceships, cruising around the galaxy with them until we are old enough to get a saucer of our own, squeezed in the back seat between two pretty girls, Aura and Borealis, while Elvis sings on the radio.

6

Beam Ships from the Pleiades

The Integratron sits on the edge of Landers, California at the place where the paved street ends and the desert road to Giant Rock begins. It is more than the desert road that links the thirty-eight-foot dome with Giant Rock, however. It was while under the rock, in the dark and cool hollow used as the center of his extraterrestrial channeling, that Van Tassel first conceived the Integratron. Built with information gained from his contact with the Space Brothers, and from his channeling of the spirit of Nikola Tesla, the Integratron's construction occupied Van Tassel's time, money, and energy for eighteen years. According to Van Tassel, the architecture and location of the Integratron would allow the structure to provide physical and spiritual rejuvenation to any who entered. He also claimed that the building would facilitate the contact with alien intelligences upon other planets and human spirits from the past and future. Unfortunately, Van Tassel died before the Integratron was completed.

Today the Integratron and its surrounding buildings are enclosed by a chain-link fence and the driveway is blocked by a pad-locked gate. When I pulled my car off the street I noticed a sign on the fence informing me that the Integratron was closed. Since I was on time for a previously scheduled appointment for a sound bath I hoped that the sign did not apply to me, though even if it did I was determined to get inside. I began to honk my car horn. After a while my incessant noisemaking seemed to get someone's attention.

7. *George Van Tassel's Integratron near Landers, California. The Integratron employs alien technology to rejuvenate the atomic structure of those who enter.*

The young woman who approached the gate informed me of what the sign had already made clear, the Integratron was closed. Barefoot and dressed in tattered blue jeans she stood on the inside of the locked gate looking out, as if the fact of the locked gate was as much out of her control as it was mine. I told her that I had an appointment for a sound bath. She said that was impossible because 'the sisters' were away for the day and only they could give a sound bath. I said that I had driven a long way to see the Integratron and didn't really need a sound bath as I had showered that morning. She did not think this was funny, but said she would go and see what she could do.

After a few minutes she returned with an older man who was carrying a ring of keys. He unlocked the gate and motioned for me to bring the car inside. As soon as I was through the gate, I saw him close it back again, padlock and all. I was now on the same side of the fence as my barefoot friend and with as little control over the gate as she had. The man with the keys walked back toward the building from which he had come. The girl, now my tour guide, motioned for me to follow her to the Integratron.

UFO religion

The exterior of the Integratron, painted a stark white, stands in contrast to its desert setting, looking for all the world like an extra-terrestrial craft that landed on earth and decided to stay, or like some 1950s version of what a human dwelling on the moon or Mars might look like in the future. The inside of the building is very different, however. Its walls and ceilings are natural wood. The ground-floor room is marked by a central column, natural wood intertwined with a striking floor-to-ceiling stripe of red. The ceiling is covered with copper wire, strung from one nail head to another, like a spider's web. A steep staircase takes you to the second floor; small windows all around the room fill it with a warm and natural glow. The domed ceiling, made of wood panels and ribbed by wooden beams, makes one think of both a church sanctuary and the interior of some sort of rocket ship, though a strange rocket ship indeed, made of wood and as warm and inviting as a country cottage.

As I walked across the floor of the upper room the sounds of my footsteps bounced from floor to ceiling and wall to wall, the echo making my lone presence sound like a crowd. Intrigued, I whistled softly, and heard echoing whispers from every direction. Along one wall I saw a set of crystal bowls of various sizes. Now I understood the sound bath. If someone had played the crystal bowls, in this room the sound would have been unbelievable. A bath of sound: that is what it would have been like. I was sorry that I missed the sisters, sorry that I missed the sound bath, sorry that I had made the joke about having taken a shower that morning. But I could not feel anything other than amusement for long while, standing under the dome of the Integratron, just across the desert sands from Giant Rock, whistling softly and snapping my fingers in time. I was a one-man band. There was applause when I finished. My barefoot guide clapping softly behind my back provided an echoing ovation. I took a bow.

Who would have guessed? Van Tassel's rejuvenation machine really works!

8. *The interior of the Integratron near Landers, California. This domed echo chamber provides the setting for sound baths.*

—The Ashtar Command —

The Integratron, as it was originally envisioned by Van Tassel, would have drawn its power from Giant Rock itself, the rock providing an electromagnetic connection to the source of universal power. The Integratron, collecting static electricity from the desert air, would literally recharge human cells, restoring their integrity and prolonging the life of all who passed through its doors. With prolonged life spans it would be possible for earthlings to acquire spiritual maturity in fewer incarnations.

It was while meditating at Giant Rock that Van Tassel received the plans for the Integratron and it was there that he made contact with a representative of the Council of Seven Lights. In July, 1952 a message from 'Ashtar, commandant quadra sector, patrol station Schare, all projections, all waves' ('Ashtar: Early Communications to George Van Tassel', 1999, available at Ministry of Universal Wisdom, http://wwwuser.gwdg.de/~agruens/UFO/ufo_apdx/ashtar_muw.html) emphasized the dangers associated with the hydrogen bomb. Van Tassel was instructed to share Ashtar's warnings with the governments of the planet of 'Shan', Ashtar's name for earth. Later, when it appeared that Ashtar's warnings concerning the hydrogen bomb had been ignored, Van Tassel was informed that the central galactic government was prepared to take special and unique steps to ensure that earth, or Shan, did no harm to the galactic unity. To make matters worse, according to Ashtar another planet in the solar system, the planet Lucifer, had destroyed itself through similar means and against the wishes of the council. They did not intend to let such a thing happen again. Van Tassel received the following message on January 23, 1953 just two and a half months after the US detonated a hydrogen bomb in the South Pacific.

> I am Ashar, commandant Vela Quadra sector, station Schare. As we informed you, our center has authorized 3 sub-station within the vortices of your planet Shan. Each of these stations now are in a position to release five hundred thousand ventalas each. Our center instructs me to inform you that you are once again about to see the use of atomic weapons in warfare. I am further requested to extend our gratitude to you for maintaining this

contact vibration. In the Light of true Love and peace, I am Ashtar.

And again in February of 1953.

> Hail in love and peace. I am Ashtar, Commandant Vela Quadra sector, station Schare. You have just heard the authority granted by Schonling Lord God of the 3rd dimensional sector, for our authority to take corrective measures. We are crating [sic] a Light energy vortices near the planet Shan in an effort to stabilize your planet. This effort requires the combined forces of 86 projections, 9100 waves, of 236,000 ventlas. Needless to say this vortices is going to create extensive damage to counteract the unbalance man has created on Shan. Our center extends to your their love and blessings. My Light, I am Ashtar.

In March of the same year Ashtar seemed even more serious.

> In love and peace, I am Ashtar. I extend through to you from our center the love and blessings for the service you have extended in maintaining this contact. I am authorized to inform you, we are in constant communication with our people, we have in your national capitol. You will be hearing of an increase of phenomena resulting in many hallucinations by your people, so called. We have been in your immediate vicinity. I repeat. Do not be alarmed by unusual occurrences around you. We are now over Mississippi River and now we arrive over your city of San Francisco. It is not our purpose to bring you continual reports of destruction ahead. Man has created his own destructive rotational Shan is in a terrible state. From our center we have activated 3 and half million primary units around this planet. Our plans are taking shape. Be prepared for anything. My love, I am Ashtar.

Though Ashtar could not stop the people of earth from detonating hydrogen bombs, perhaps his people were helpful in limiting the effects and with ensuring that all-out war did not break out upon the planet.

Van Tassel's relationship with Ashtar was not to be an exclusive one. Because of Van Tassel's stature in contactee circles the idea of the 'Ashtar Command,' or an organization dedicated to the enforcement of galactic law, became a common theme in many contactee accounts. Van Tassel's one-time partner Robert Short broke with him in an attempt to make the movement more popular. In 1955 Elouise Moeller channeled Ashtar and revealed that ships from the command would soon land on earth in great numbers. She was but the tip of the iceberg in terms of those who claimed to have been in contact with Ashtar or with some other member of his organization. One of the most important of these was Tuella (Thelma B. Terrill), who in the 1970s and 1980s brought Ashtar to the attention of a whole new audience.

Tuella, with a significant background in the Theosophical movement, brought a much more spiritual message from Ashtar than had Van Tassel. She reported, like Moeller, that a fleet of ships from the Ashtar Command was on its way to earth to evacuate a select few humans in anticipation of a world-wide crisis. Later, however, Tuella's emphasis would focus more on the spiritual side of Ashtar's message and far less on the literal. As Christopher Helland notes:

> She spoke less of physical UFOs and increasingly emphasized the spiritual nature of liberation and the religious teachings of Ashtar. In effect, she transferred the Ashtar movement to mainstream theosophical spirituality. . . . [In her later publications] she teaches that the human race must make an ascension or transition to a more spiritual state of existence if it is to survive. The idea of a literal evacuation of the Earth is explicitly downplayed as being 'a most difficult task to carry out in lift of all that would be involved.' (Christopher Helland, 'From Extraterrestrials to Ultraterrestrials: The Evolution of the Concept of Ashtar', in Partridge, 2003: 172–3)

Though Tuella transitioned from a literal to a spiritual interpretation of Ashtar's message, not everyone in the Ashtar Command movement would do so. Yvonne Cole, for example, predicted that the Ashtar Command fleet would arrive on earth in 1994. In preparation for the great event she trained her followers to perform tasks that would assist the fleet with its mission. When the fleet failed to materialize in 1994 Cole's prophecy joined a long list of failed predictions. It was another mark against the literalist version of the Ashtar Command and another mark in favor of Tuella's spiritualization of the doctrine.

Indeed, as Helland has persuasively argued, the contemporary form of the Ashtar Command movement is clearly more related to

Theosophy than was Van Tassel's original teachings. Ashtar is now regarded as more than just a glorified Captain Kirk. He is in reality much closer to Jesus in status and importance. As Helland notes, the latest version of the Ashtar Command movement believes

> that there are millions of spaceships constantly in the vicinity of the Earth, but that those 'guardianships' would never intervene on the planet's surface, unless there was a serious problem such as a third world war or an 'astrophysical catastrophe'. An analysis of messages reveals that Ashtar's influence is becoming increasingly subtle: e.g. 'encouraging the shift from fossil fuel to free energy, and non-polluting energy sources and transportation.' (in Partridge, 2003: 175)

It simply is not the case that all literal interpretations of Ashtar Command have disappeared, however, a fact that Helland makes clear. A recent claim of flights aboard extraterrestrial spacecraft is itself something of a spiritual claim, however.

> In 1994 a small group of Ashtar Command members claimed that an extraordinary event had taken place: 'the lift-off experience.' What they communicated through the Ashtar network was that they had been taken off Earth and placed aboard the 'ships of Light' that were circling the planet. . . . This involved the human consciousness (or, sometimes, the 'etheric body') being raised from the physical dimension and transferred to the 'Light ships.' (in Partridge, 2003: 176)

In addition, those who had participated in the first experience revealed that it was to be repeated in December of that year. According to Helland,

> Over 250 people participated in the second 'lift-off experience', the successful outcome of which was immediately declared by the leadership: 'In manifesting the 2nd Voyage, we have opened a portal to the AC [Ashtar Command] Ships forever.' By claiming that a portal had been opened, anyone involved with the Ashtar Command could now theoretically 'raise their vibration' in order to be transported to these extraterrestrial vessels. (in Partridge, 2003: 176)

The popularity of the lift-off experience has continued to grow. Websites provide the opportunity for participants to share their experiences with one another. Spaceships and their crew are described in detail. And, since time does not flow at the same speed aboard the fast-moving craft as it does upon the earth, a few minutes of meditation provides enough earth time for an extended visit aboard ship.

Perhaps my moment of reverie under the dome of the Integratron was even more significant than I thought. Perhaps in that split second I was transported aboard a spacecraft in orbit around the earth. Perhaps the applause wasn't for my whistling at all, but for the successful completion of some critical and dangerous mission. I never was that good at whistling.

— Aetherius —

George King reported his first contact with an extraterrestrial entity to have occurred in London in 1954. According to his story, King was startled by a loud, apparently physically audible voice. The voice revealed itself as Aetherius, a name later discovered to be a pseudonym for a Cosmic Master, a highly evolved extraterrestrial. Such Cosmic Masters have, on occasion, made themselves visible upon our own planet, most famously in the form of Jesus, Buddha, Krishna, and Lao Tzu. Because of the higher vibrational level occupied by such beings they cannot be detected by humans unless they choose to reveal themselves. It was thus by deliberate choice that Aetherius revealed himself to King and instructed him to 'Prepare yourself! You are to become the voice of Interplanetary Paliament.' King claims to have gone on to communicate with many other 'Cosmic Masters' including the Great White Brotherhood of Theosophy, Jesus, Buddha, and the extraterrestrial known as 'Mars Sector 6.'

King soon founded a religious organization known as the Aetherius Society and published several books expanding upon the truths he had received from Aetherius and others. King's teachings were clearly influenced by Theosophy and by eastern philosophy, facts that he never tried to deny. He emphasized the familiar themes of Theosophy and eastern religion – karma, reincarnation, contact with higher beings, and an alternative understanding of human history – more forcefully than perhaps any other contactee. He also emphasized the reality of extraterrestrial entities in contact with humans.

In his *Flying Saucers: A Report on the Flying Saucers, Their Crews, and Their Mission to Earth* (1964), King explains why extraterrestrials visit the earth. According to King, flying saucers come primarily from Mars and Venus, under the orders of the Interplanetary Parliament located on Saturn. The visitors from our two closest neighbors are here to complete a 'metaphysical survey.' One of their primary concerns is the release of radioactive material into space, which has already damaged our atmosphere. Martians and Venusians are sending into the atmosphere remotely controlled 'implosion devices' that will absorb some of the static radioactivity. This work has already prevented many terrible natural disasters from occurring. Unfortunately, the axis of the earth has already been shifted through atomic explosions. This has altered the earth's 'lines of magnetic force' and may lead to molecular mutations in human cellular structure.

The mother-ships operated by our spacefaring neighbors are shaped like cigars. They can carry seven to nine scout patrol ships. These patrol ships are the type of craft most commonly reported in UFO sightings. They look like the traditional notion of a flying saucer, indeed they look very much like the scout ships photographed by Adamski. These craft can be made invisible at will by changing their vibrational level. This explains a commonly reported aspect of flying saucer behavior.

In addition to the mother-ships and the scout ships, King revealed that a third type of ship is sometimes employed. These ships are only employed by the Great Cosmic Masters and can likewise be made visible or invisible. The Great Cosmic Masters are the Ancient Ones of the solar system and are in control of all human life throughout the Milky Way. One of these vessels was made visible to the inhabitants of the earth in ancient times when some of the masters needed to approach near the earth to complete the complicated operations associated with the conception of Jesus. Thus the star of Bethlehem was in reality one of these special spacecraft.

The occupants of the flying saucers look very much like humans when they choose to become visible. According to King, these residents of Venus, Mars, Jupiter, and Saturn have a much finer skin texture and bone structure than do residents of the earth. Indeed, the extraterrestrial visitors look very much like the Eastern Saints of Theosophy. Usually these extraterrestrial visitors wear one-piece suits that protect them from the bacteria in our atmosphere. These beings do not eat, but receive energy directly from the sun.

More important than these details about flying saucers and their crew, however, is the central message of Master Aetherius.

> Man is a Holy Spirit, living upon an Earth which, because of the Divine Mind which fashioned it, is also Holy. If we accept this in every phase of its meaning we have made a vital step toward the realization of ONE-NESS. For then we will be prepared to live as brothers in one of the rooms of the 'Many Mansions.' No longer will this Earth of ours be a prison but a temple in which we can make loving sacrifice for one another. A Holy Temple with an ever open door, through which we can come and go at will. (Lewis, 2003: 403)

This realization of the unity of all reality is the central message of the many great religious teachers of the past. In this sense Master Aetherius makes no claim to a unique message. King quotes the Master as saying, 'Whether you are a follower of Mohammed, Buddha, or Jesus, it is up to you to LIVE the teachings of your Master. Choose a Master whose teachings seem right for you and learn, understand, and LIVE THOSE TEACHINGS' (in Lewis, 2003: 403). Thus the ability to transform one's self as well as the entire earth resides in each individual through the teachings of the Great Masters.

> Every man and woman who reads this has the ability to speed up their evolution that together they can become a tremendous power for good in this world. A Power strong enough to outlaw war and murder forever. Every one of you can start it now – today – by modeling your lives upon the dedicated lives of those Masters Who sacrificed Planetary Heaven for your benefit.
> 'You are not alone in your struggles . . . you never have been alone. Every step you take toward the Great Masters, they will take two toward you.'
> THIS IS THE MOST WONDERFUL NEWS OF MODERN TIMES!
> For, when Aetherius made this simple but nevertheless profound statement, He gave the gospel and guarantee as did that

other Venusian Who chose to be born the son of a village carpenter, two thousand years ago . . . (in Lewis, 2003: 404)

The future for those who accept and follow the teachings of the Great Masters is bright indeed. Humans from earth will find that they can share in the blessed existence of the space brothers: 'You will no longer be confined to this Earth but will live as befits the Cosmic Beings which you have then become. The Planets will be your 'holiday' resorts. You will speak a thousand tongues in a thousand different worlds' (Lewis, 2003: 403).

You know, this sounds pretty good to me. Since I was a kid I have been dreaming of vacationing on other planets. That was what we were promised, wasn't it? Just be patient and in a few years technology will allow you to travel through space in your family cruiser. I distinctly remember that when I was in elementary school the Space Shuttle was sold to us as a space taxi, implying to my seven-year-old self that you should be able to flag one down on the corner and, for a fare, be transported to Mars. I can see it now: cocktails on Venus, dinner and dancing on Jupiter, and then back to the Moon for a nightcap, a Martian Martini perhaps, or a Cosmic Cosmopolitan. The night is still young.

— Urantia Foundation —

According to the orthodox history of the Urantia Brotherhood, the first communications between their founder, William Sadler, and his extraterrestrial contacts took place between 1906 and 1911. (For a contrasting view of the book's origins see Martin Gardner's *Urantia: The Great Cult Mystery*). These contacts occurred through the medium of a 'sleeping subject,' one of Dr. Sadler's psychiatric patients who would enter into trance-like states. On the occasion of the first contact the patient spoke while in the sleep state, though in a voice very different from the patient's own that identified itself as a being from another planet on an observation mission. In the years that followed the sleeping subject would channel the presence of many such visitors.

In 1925 the method of communication changed when the sleeping subject reported that he had discovered a mysterious handwritten document in his home. Over time Sadler and the 'Forum,' a group of individuals who were privy to the sleeping subject's contact experiences, would obtain an incredible amount of information through these student visitors, mostly by asking them questions. This group met and recorded revelations throughout 1942. The record of their conversations with the extraterrestrial contacts was published in 1955 as *The Urantia Book*. After that all communication with the extraterrestrials ceased.

According to official Urantia Foundation statements the central message of *The Urantia Book* is the unity of all human beings as sons and daughters of the one God. It details the origin, history, and destiny of humanity and provides a unique interpretation of the teachings of Jesus in which the truth of humanity's ascension to the Universal Father is revealed. *The Urantia Book* does not advocate a new organized religion, but rather builds upon the religions of the past and present.

The book is divided into four parts. Part One details the nature of the Central and Superuniverse and explains the nature of God, the reality of Paradise, the organization of the Central and Superuniverse, the personalities of the Grand Universe, and the destiny of mortals. Part Two is concerned with the Local Universe and creation of a son of the 'Paradise Order of Michael.' The local universe is made up of one hundred constellations, each comprised of one hundred systems of inhabited worlds. Each of these systems will, upon completion, contain one thousand inhabited spheres. The earth, known as Urantia, is part of a local universe ruled by Michael, known on Urantia as Jesus Christ.

The third part of *The Urantia Book* provides the history of Urantia itself. One billion years ago Urantia attained its present size and was placed on the registry of our local universe and given the name Urantia. The planet is a unique and special place to the inhabitants of our local universe, being the physical birthplace of Michael. Part Four focuses upon the life and teachings of Michael/Jesus. Occupying the last part of the book, the life of Jesus is presented as the climax of the evolution of the universe. 'The great hope of Urantia lies in the possibility of a new revelation of Jesus with a new and enlarged presentation of his saving message which would spiritually unite in loving service the numerous families of his present day professed followers' (Urantia Foundation, 1955: 2086:2).

Urantia is starting to bring me down. This is all a little bit boring. *The Urantia Book*'s detailed analysis of galactic politics leave me cold. It is more than a little like watching the *Star Wars* prequels and wondering who the hell cares about the space senate and the galactic peace treaty and who has been elected to be galactic mumbo-jumbo over what planet. Well I guess that is what one should expect when the primary contacts are made through a man who was sound asleep. Maybe I'll pick up *The Urantia Book* again and see if I can doze off, catch a few zzzzs, open up my own sleep channel to the stars.

— Unarius —

Unarius was founded in 1954 by Ernest Norman and his wife Ruth. Both are regarded by their followers as cosmic visionaries charged with bringing the truth of evolutionary physics to the world. Between 1954 and the time of Ernest's death in 1971 the Normans authored several books and attracted a small following. After Ernest's death, however, the movement underwent a sort of revival. Under Ruth's leadership Unarius was given a permanent home in El Cajon, California from where she operated the Center for New World Teaching. Ruth also founded Unarius centers at various locations around the world.

In addition to strengthening the institution of Unarius, Ruth brought a decidedly more charismatic style of leadership to the organization. Dressing in elaborate gowns and crowned with tiaras, Ruth looked more like Glenda the Good Witch of the North than like a representative of a galactic federation. However, her gentle and loving persona was certainly an element in the growth of Unarius under her leadership. Ruth herself died in 1993, leaving a charismatic void that has not yet been filled.

The teachings of Unarius are reminiscent of other UFO movements. According to John A. Saliba ('UFOs and Religion: A Case Study of Unarius', in Lewis, 2003) they can be grouped into four main beliefs. First, Unarius believes in the existence of intelligent life on other planets and in other parts of our galaxy. Like other saucer groups, Unarius describes these beings as humanoids, some of whom may have lived upon this world in past lives. The vast majority of these beings are more advanced than humans. Extraterrestrials visit the earth, according to the Unarians, for reasons that we have heard before; they wish to assist the earth in avoiding radiation poisoning and they wish to assist humans in their evolution to higher states. Second, Unarius believes in a limitless creator. This creator tends to be thought of as an impersonal force to which one may relate in a type of spiritual oneness.

Third, Unarius believes that humans are engaged in a process of evolving reincarnation. The goal of this process is a familiar one, the participation in the life of cosmic humanity. The strategy for achieving this is somewhat unique, however, for it involves extensive past life therapy. In order for humans to reach the next stage of evolution they must first come to understand their past incarnations. For example, through past life regression Ruth Norman came to understand the dynamics of her previous life experiences, Ernest's true identity as Raphiel, and her own identity as the Archangel Uriel. Both Raphiel and Uriel have worked through many lifetimes for the good of humanity. In previous lives Ruth was Socrates, Peter the Great, Charlemagne, Queen Elizabeth I, Queen Maria Theresa, Hatshepsut, Quetzalcoatl, and Mary of Bethany, the betrothed and thirteenth disciple of Jesus, who was himself an earlier incarnation of Ernest.

The fourth central belief of the Unarius movement is their belief in the future arrival of extraterrestrial visitors to our planet. A starship carrying one thousand scientists from a planet known as Myton in the constellation of the Pleiades will descend to the earth and land in the ocean on a rising landmass that was once the continent of Atlantis. The Muon scientists from Myton will introduce technology to cleanse the air and restore the planet to its original purity. They will also serve as examples for other humans in their behavior and love for one another. A landing that had been predicted for 2001 was cancelled because the people of earth were not yet prepared to receive the truths offered by the space people. This failure was at least in part the responsibility of Unarius students. According to the official Unarius website (www.unarius.org):

Many Unarius students have recognized that they have been the planetary leaders in past civilizations. As these leaders they have not been receptive to the advanced masters who lived amongst them to teach a higher understanding of life. The students at Star Center One in El Cajon have been reliving a lifetime when their negative consciousness and insane acts interfered with the forward progression of planet Earth. In this past lifetime in ancient Egypt, they turned against their teachers, the great spiritual leaders Osiris and Isis, brutally murdering them just as their Space Brothers were about to land on Earth to take Isis and Osiris back to their home planet. Upon seeing what had befallen their brothers, the spaceship flew away. It was evident that the angry, crazed mob didn't want the Space Brothers to land. The cover-up of what happened over 10,000 years ago was so pervasive that there are no historical records of Osiris and Isis, other than that they were mythical gods of ancient Egypt.

Of course, Isis and Osiris were earlier incarnations of Ruth and Ernest.

When the landing does take place, earth will be invited to be the thirty-third member of the Interplanetary Confederation. When earth is ready to accept the offer, thirty-three spaceships with ambassadors from all Confederation planets will land together at the Unarius landing site and form Unarius Star Center One, an interplanetary university.

Okay, Unarius – one, Urantia – zero. This is good stuff. Uriel dressed in intergalactic gowns helps her followers relive their past lives. Representatives of thirty-three planets to land in Southern California and found a university. The Unarians also have annual parades with women wearing tights and capes and blowing trumpets. Did I mention the 1969 Cadillac with a flying saucer mounted on the roof?

— Billy Meier —

Eduard 'Billy' Meier claims that his first alien contact occurred when he was five years old. These contacts have continued throughout his life but reached their climax with the eleven-year period of contact with the Pleiadian named Semjase that began in 1975. It was at this point that Meier began to understand most fully his mission as the prophet of the truth. In 1977, he founded the Semjase Silver Star Center in Switzerland on a farm where he still lives with a rotating group of followers and seekers.

Meier's extraterrestrial contacts have taken three forms. First, he has had personal face-to face contacts with the extraterrestrials. The usual instigation of these contacts is through telepathically received information concerning the time and place of the meeting. Meier walks to the location or, if it is far away, he travels by moped, car, or tractor. Meier is instructed to go alone to these meetings, though he is allowed to have a friend drive him most of the way as long as he walks the final distance alone. He may also be led to the destination through a sort of guidance. In this case he leaves home and follows the extraterrestrial signals to the location. On occasion he has also been teleported from one spot to another in order to greet the visitors. Once at the site Meier simply stands under the hovering spacecraft and is lifted, as if by invisible elevator, into the craft. Once inside the craft Billy is able to interact physically with the visitors.

The second form of contact is through telepathy, in which Billy sends and receives mental messages from the extraterrestrials. The third form is through inspirations; in this case Meier is able to receive messages but is not able to send them. Billy's experience with extraterrestrials is documented through an extensive collection of photographs, making him in that respect closely related to George Adamski. While Adamski's photos were reported to be scout ships from Venus, however, Meier identifies the objects in his photographs as beam ships from the Pleiades.

An excellent account of Pleiadians can be found in *And Still They Fly!* by Guido Moosbrugger (2004). Moosbrugger tells us that Meier's contacts come to earth from the section of space identified with the Pleiades, a star cluster visible from earth. The beings known by Meier as the Pleiadians are from the same region of the sky but from another space–time configuration and eighty light years beyond the Pleiades themselves. Meier has called them Pleiadians because their home world lies in the direction of the Pleiades and because the name used by the extraterrestrials when referring to themselves sounds like the term Pleiades. They are, in reality, the Plejaren.

Meier has been in contact with a good number of the Plejaren, though the three main personalities are Ptaah, Semjase, and Quetzal. Ptaah is, according to Moosbrugger's account, 770 years old and the commander of the Pleiadian space fleet. His title is JHWH, which means king of wisdom. Semjase is 344 years old and holds the rank of half-Jschrjsch, or half-queen of wisdom or half-goddess. Semjase suffered an accident in 1977 at the Star Center and had to return to her home planet. She returned some six months later and continued to contact Meier through to 1984, when a related illness sent her home once more. Quetzal is 464 years of age and is commander of the Pleiadian stations in our solar system.

Meier has learned that the Pleiadians and humans are descended from common ancestors from the Lyra and Vega systems. Members of this ancestral race visited the earth in the ancient past when our more immediate human progenitors were in a primitive state of development. Because of the evil actions of this ancestor race, and because of human complicity with these actions, much suffering and pain was introduced into the world. Thus the visits by Lyrans and Vegans brought many negative things to the primitive earthers. They also, however, brought advances in civilization and technology that catapulted humans into the advanced position we are in today. Revered as gods, these beings people the ancient myths and legends of our world.

The Pleiadians, in this way like Adamski's Venusians, are visiting our planet in an attempt to remedy some of the symptoms of humanity's spiritual immaturity. They offer warnings that they have entrusted to Billy Meier to communicate to the world. Such warnings concern human overpopulation, the destruction of the ozone layer, the threat of nuclear energy, the exploitation of the earth's resources, and plans of wars and conquests.

In addition to these warnings, however, the Pleiadians also offer prophecies concerning the future of our planet. For example, it is predicted that there will be a discovery of ancient alien artifacts on the planet Mars. A new DNA code will be discovered that will revolutionize health care and greatly extend the human life span. Human beings will, in the future, be converted into robot-like machines. Scientists will also create animal–human hybrids. The 'semi-human' hybrids will declare unity with the robotic humans because of their common state.

> [Scientists] will be creating entities, so called semi-humans, whom they will produce by cross-breeding human beings with pigs and then train them as fighting machines. These entities will be sent to war and also perform a variety of tasks in space. However, this situation will not go well for very long. The entities will oppose their creators, as is also the case with the robotic humans who will have had arms and legs amputated so their nervous systems can be attached to minute electronic-biological devices, whereby these semi-humans will become living navigational devices or spaceships and every type of weaponry, machinery, and earth vehicles, to name but a few. (Moosbrugger, 2004: 298)

Of course, this does not have to be the destiny of the human race. As Quetzal once informed Billy:

> I would like to point out that prophecies are always changeable and can be changed for the better if man makes positive changes in his thoughts, feelings, and actions leading to that which is better and positively progressive. Prophecies always rest upon specific causes: these again result in certain effects, whereby these effects can be changed at any time if only the preceding causes are changed in their form. Therefore it is possible that negative or evil prophecies do not have to be fulfilled, if the preceding causes will be purposely changed in a manner, that positive and good develops instead of negative and evil. (Moosbrugger, 2004: 307)

Thus the role of Billy Meier, prophet of truth, is to assist in the transformation of human consciousness and behavior so that he may effect the transformation of human future.

But I say, 'Why change the future?' Half-human/half-robots teamed with half-human/half-animal hybrids sound pretty cool to me.

— Heaven's Gate —

Marshall Herff Applewhite and Bonnie Lu Nettles met in 1972. Nettles was at that time involved in Theosophy and channeling, which she introduced to Applewhite. Shortly after their meeting they left Houston together. In 1973 Applewhite identified himself and Nettles as the two prophets of the Book of Revelation. According to the biblical account, the prophets would be killed and then rise to heaven in a cloud, just as Jesus had done at his ascension; Applewhite believed that the cloud was symbolic of a flying saucer. After a while Applewhite and Nettles began to call themselves Bo and Peep. They first caught the public's attention in 1975 when some thirty people were reported as missing following a lecture by Applewhite in Walport, Oregon. It was correctly assumed that the missing persons had left with Applewhite. Most of those, and others who joined the group later, would not stay for long. Bo and Peep never attracted a large following, perhaps reaching a maximum of 150 or so during the late 1970s. By the mid-1980s Bo and Peep seemed to have given up trying to attract a large following and began to focus on the special and unique role that was required of their followers.

The teachings of Bo and Peep centered on extraterrestrial entities who had last visited the earth some 2,000 years ago. Deciding that humans at that time were not yet ready to ascend to the 'level above human' they left one of their number behind and went on their way. According to the Heaven's Gate website:

> Two thousand years ago, a crew of members of the Kingdom of Heaven who are responsible for nurturing 'gardens,' determined that a percentage of the human 'plants' of the present civilization of this Garden (Earth) had developed enough that some of those bodies might be ready to be used as 'containers' for soul deposits. Upon instruction, a member of the Kingdom of Heaven then left behind His body in that Next Level (similar to putting it in a closet, like a suit of clothes that doesn't need to be worn for awhile), came to Earth, and moved into (or incarnated into), an adult human body (or 'vehicle') that had been 'prepped' for this particular task. The body that was chosen was called Jesus. The member of the Kingdom of Heaven who was instructed to incarnate into that body did so at His 'Father's' (or Older Member's) instruction. He 'moved into' (or took over) that body when it was 29 or 30 years old, at the time referred to as its baptism by John the Baptist (the incarnating event was depicted as '. . . the Holy Spirit descended upon Him in bodily form like a dove' – Luke 3:22). (That body (named Jesus) was tagged in its formative period to be the receptacle of a Next Level Representative, and

even just that 'tagging' gave that 'vehicle' some unique awareness of its coming purpose.) (http://religiousmovements.lib.
virginia.edu/nrms/heavensgate_mirror/index.html)

Bo and Peep came to see themselves as extraterrestrials who had
been left on earth as Jesus had to prepare the world for the next stage
of evolution.

> Our mission is exactly the same. I am in the same position to
> today's society as was the One that was in Jesus then. My being
> here now is actually a continuation of that last task as was prom-
> ised, to those who were students 2000 years ago. They are here
> again, continuing in their own overcoming, while offering the
> same transition to others. Our only purpose is to offer the disci-
> pline and 'grafting' required of this transition into membership
> in My Father's House. My Father, my Older Member, came with
> me this time for the first half of this task to assist in the task
> because of its present difficulty. . . . The dilemma is we are here
> and most humans are thoroughly 'hooked' to humanity. How-
> ever, the same 'grace' that was available at the end of the
> Representative's mission 2000 years ago is available now with
> our presence. If you quickly choose to take these steps toward
> separating from the world, and look to us for help, you will see
> our Father's Kingdom.

Bo and Peep developed a complex set of behavior rules in order
to assist their followers to achieve Human Individual Metamor-
phisis. Their followers were required to change their names and cut
their hair. They were required to abandon all earthly connections
and to abstain from lust and sex. Late in the movement, Applewhite
and some of his followers went so far as to have themselves cas-
trated in order to gain control of their desires. In 1997 as the comet
Halle-Bopp approached the earth, Applewhite announced that the
spaceship was approaching, hiding from earth telescopes in the
comet's tail. On March 29, 1997, thirty-nine members of the group,
including Applewhite (Nettles died of natural causes before the
event), were found dead in their Southern California home. They
were dressed in matching clothes and matching shoes. Apparently
they had committed suicide as a means of leaving the earth and joining the Space Brothers who were coming for them.

Few outsiders had looked at the Heaven's Gate website in the days before their deaths but all the clues concerning what was about to happen were there. Applewhite wrote,

> A member of the Kingdom of God – the Evolutionary Level Above Human – I, who am called Do, acknowledge that:
> I am about to return to my Father's Kingdom. This 'return' requires that I prepare to lay down my borrowed human body in order to take up, or reenter, my body (biological) belonging to the Kingdom of God (as I did approximately 2000 years ago, as Jesus, when I laid down the human body that was about 33 years old in order to reenter my body belonging to the Kingdom of Heaven).

Likewise, Applewhite's followers:

> The students/disciples who successfully bond to the Level Above Human through me and my Father must also prepare to lay down their human bodies as we go to the Kingdom of Heaven, in order to take up bodies appropriate to and belonging to that more advanced Kingdom Level.

Applewhite also wrote:

> Hale-Bopp's approach is the 'marker' we've been waiting for – the time for the arrival of the spacecraft from the Level Above Human to take us home to 'Their World' – in the literal Heavens. Our 22 years of classroom here on planet Earth is finally coming to conclusion – 'graduation' from the Human Evolutionary Level. We are happily prepared to leave 'this world' and go with Ti's crew.

Applewhite expected their departure to be physical. That is, he expected to physically board the coming space craft.

> We fully desire, expect, and look forward to boarding a space-craft from the Next Level very soon (in our physical bodies). There is no doubt in our mind that our being 'picked up' is inevitable in the very near future. But what happens between now and then is the big question. We are keenly aware of several possibilities.
> It could happen that before that spacecraft comes, one or more of us could lose our physical vehicles (bodies) due to 'recall,' accident, or at the hands of some irate individual. We do not anticipate this, but it is possible. Another possibility is that,

because of the position we take in our information, we could find so much disfavor with the powers that control this world that there could be attempts to incarcerate us or to subject us to some sort of psychological or physical torture (such as occurred at both Ruby Ridge and Waco).

Then,

It has always been our way to examine all possibilities, and be mentally prepared for whatever may come our way. For example, consider what happened at Masada around 73 A.D. A devout Jewish sect, after holding out against a siege by the Romans, to the best of their ability, and seeing that the murder, rape, and torture of their community was inevitable, determined that it was permissible for them to evacuate their bodies by a more dignified, and less agonizing method. We have thoroughly discussed this topic (of willful exit of the body under such conditions), and have mentally prepared ourselves for this possibility (as can be seen in a few of our statements). However, this act certainly does not need serious consideration at this time, and hopefully will not in the future.

◆　◆　◆

Heaven's Gate is a long way from the Integratron, a long way from those conventions at Giant Rock, a long way from Van Tassel's dream of extending human life spans in order to provide an opportunity for personal transformation and growth. Heaven's Gate ended badly. It became something different to the contactee movements it so resembles. It became a 'cult' in the worst sense of that term.

The topic of this chapter differs from the previous one in that the focus is on organized religious groups and movements rather than individual contactees. The difference between Adamski/Bethurum/Angelucci and Van Tassel/King/Meier is that the former claimed to have been contacted by extraterrestrials, but this claim was never successfully transformed into an organized religious movement. In greater and lesser degrees, this is precisely what the latter group managed to accomplish. Van Tassel's Ashtar Command, King's Aetherius Society, and Applewhite's Heaven's Gate are all organized groups focused around the claims of a central contactee. Of course this doesn't mean that all such groups are by definition dangerous. Such depends on a whole host of other factors, not the least of which is the personalities of the individuals, both leaders and followers, who make up that group.

The teachings of Heaven's Gate did not differ all that much from the teachings of other contactee organizations nor, for that matter, of the Adamski-era contactees themselves. However, in place of the openness to others that is a common theme espoused by those claiming contact with extraterrestrials, Heaven's Gate was a closed society, suspicious of the external world. In place of the kooky fun of most contactees, Heaven's Gate was deadly serious. Unlike Ruth Norman's transformation into a galactic queen upon the death of her beloved Ernest, Herff Applewhite never recovered from the death of Bonnie Lu Nettles; Bo lost his Peep and did not know where to find her. Shaved heads led to castration, which led to suicide. Unlike most other contactee groups, and practically all of the individual contactees, Heaven's Gate found little that was good in human nature, little that could give them hope. What hope they had was thought to be coming from above, a starship in a comet's tail. They had given up on transforming the world, the best they could do was to escape it.

PART THREE

History's Mysteries

7

Ancient Astronauts

My grandmother was a witness to the apocalypse. Born between the American Civil War and World War I she must have known about warfare, even if it was only from stories told by veterans. Raised in the southern United States at a time after Reconstruction and before the New Deal she must have been aware of the march of technological progress, even if she lived without electricity or indoor plumbing for most of her life. I never met my grandmother; she was old when my father was born, the last of her nine children; my father was old when I was born, the last of four. I cannot imagine what she must have been like. I cannot imagine the world that she inhabited, the way that she lived, the things that made her wonder and dream.

There is one story that is told about my grandmother in my family, it must have taken place in the late 1950s or early 1960s, that makes her feel at once very far away from me and, inexplicably, very close. The story tells of the day a fleet of National Guard helicopters landed in a field next to her home. The sound was deafening, probably bringing to mind the terror of a tornado. The wind from the giant rotors shook the windows and rattled the pots and pans in the cabinets. When my grandmother found enough courage to look out the door she knew immediately what was happening.

This was her apocalypse. The locusts from the Book of Revelation, the beasts from the pit, were upon her. The end was here. For certain she had known of war, for certain she had known of machines and technology. This, however, was beyond her knowledge, beyond her experience. This was the end of the world.

— Moundville —

Standing atop the huge mound on the banks of the Black Warrior River in Alabama it is hard to imagine the valley below as it once was. The surrounding, smaller mounds would have been topped by houses and filled with activity. In the low places surrounding the mounds were gardens, refuse dumps, and the homes of the less wealthy, less important members of the city. Smoke from the fires would have filled the air. At one time the now-empty mounds located in the appropriately named town of Moundville, Alabama formed one of the largest cities in North America, part of the great Mississippian culture that was already in decline when Hernando De Soto explored the American wilderness. The only things remaining to mark what once was there are the earthen mounds rising above the flood plain. I feel strange when I visit Moundville, as if it were inhabited by ghosts, no, not ghosts but something stranger. Ghosts I could identify with, see-through people dressed in nineteenth-century clothing, maybe carrying a lantern or wrapped in chains. Moundville makes me feel stranger than that because I cannot imagine what these people looked like. I can't imagine how they lived or what they believed. They are even farther away from me than my grandmother, whose life I could never comprehend. The world of the mound builders is as alien as a Martian city or a Venusian village. I do not understand its customs, I do not understand its form of life, I do not understand the mounds – not their purpose nor the techniques of their construction. The people who live there might as well have lived on the moon.

When the first European settlers discovered the ancient mounds they would often simply plow them under, discovering in the process the buried remains of people from the distant past. When Europeans did stop and examine the mounds they too were intrigued by the utter mystery of their construction and their purpose, by the alienness that seems to haunt them. As Robert Silverberg, author of countless books about alien civilizations, points out in his excellent non-fiction book *The Mound Builders* (1968), Europeans were so impressed by the mounds that they could not believe that they had been built by anyone indigenous to North America. They were just too different to have been the product of any American Indian culture. Theories described the mounds as the work of the Egyptians, Greeks, Romans, Israelites, Scandinavians, Welsh, Scots, and Chinese – practically anyone other than the Native Americans. These theories were never really supported by any good evidence, of course. They were simply attempts to explain the existence of one alien thing (the mounds) with another (other ancient and mysterious civilizations). The threat of infinite regress seemed to bother no one.

Such theorizing was not only the activity of specialists, but also captured the imagination of the public. For example, the novel *Behemoth: A Legend of the Mound Builders*, published in 1839 by Cornelius Mathews, tells the story of a mound-builder city terrorized by a wooly mammoth. The story 'Centeola: The Maid of the Mounds,' published by Daniel Pierce Thompson in 1864, set a traditional romantic adventure among the people of the mounds. For every theory concerning how the Greeks or Israelites found their way to North America there was usually an account of how the savage Indians had slaughtered the great civilization that the Greeks or Israelites had built.

Of course the mounds were built by indigenous North Americans who had a much grander civilization than could have been imagined by nineteenth-century Europeans. That fact would not have fitted with the idea of the indigenous peoples as savages in need of taming or even annihilation. Over time, however, mainstream archeologists, anthropologists, and historians came to accept the idea that the mound builders were indigenous to the continent. There has remained, however, a small group of people opposed to this idea, people for whom the heights of ancient civilizations, from Egypt to North America, simply seem too alien for a good earthly explanation to suffice.

— Joseph Smith —

Joseph Smith had something in common with old Dr. Gee, of Aztec fame. They were both doodlebuggers: Dr. Gee claimed that he had used extraterrestrial technology recovered from a crashed flying saucer to locate oil wells, Jospeh Smith used a 'peep-stone' with mysterious powers to locate buried treasures, treasures buried by the ancient mound builders. According to David Persuitte in *Joseph Smith and the Origins of the Book of Mormon*

> Joseph's job was to 'search' for the treasures by using a technique similar to water dowsing, except that he used a 'peepstone' instead of a forked stick. By placing the 'peepstone' in his hat and gazing at it like a fortune teller would gaze into a crystal ball, he would 'locate' the treasure and direct the diggers where to dig. (Persuitte, 2000: 35)

In 1823 Smith gave up searching for buried treasure. In that year he claims to have experienced a visit from the Angel Moroni. Moroni instructed Smith to go to the Hill of Cumorah, itself probably an ancient Indian mound. Buried there, Smith found gold tablets written in a strange language. This was the *Book of Mormon*, a book filled with the history of the mound builders. According to the book, God sent pilgrims from the Middle East following the destruction of the Tower of Babel. Once in North America, they built great cities and mounds and developed into a prosperous civilization. They thrived until they destroyed one another in a terrible civil war.

Then, many years later in 600 BCE, God helped a number of Israelites escape before the destruction of Jerusalem and led them to America. Like their predecessors, these visitors built great cities. Unfortunately, they also split into warring factions. The Nephites were the mound builders, the Lamanites were the ancestors of the Native Americans. Because of the sins of the Nephites, God allowed the Lamanites to destroy them. Hence today only their mounds remain. The Lamanites were not sinless, however, and were marked by God with red skin and forced to live a savage, uncivilized existence. To this day many Mormon archeologists, both amateur and professional, refuse to believe the mainstream history of North America and seek evidence to support their claim that the mound builders were descendants of the ancient Israelites.

Of special interest to our study is the fact that the *Book of Mormon* and subsequent Mormon teaching, both official and unofficial, trace the ancestry of humanity in general to an extraterrestrial origin and believe that the ancient history of North America was shaped by an extraterrestrial hand. Indeed, for Latter-Day Saints, God himself is a being from another planet. The great mound builder civilization was thus built under the guiding hand of a being from space.

According to official Latter-Day Saints history, Joseph Smith acquired another ancient manuscript through extraordinary means. (Okay, maybe not so extraordinary considering the way that the *Book of Mormon* was discovered, but pretty interesting nevertheless.) According to Andrew Skinner, in 1835 several mummies were discovered in Thebes, along with two papyrus rolls and several papyrus fragments (Andrew Skinner, 'The Book of Abraham: A Most Remarkable Book,' *Ensign*, March 1997: 16). The mummies and papyri ended up in New York in the possession of Michael Chandler. Chandler had trouble finding anyone who could translate the texts for him. Hearing of Joseph Smith's ability to translate ancient texts Chandler asked him to do so. Smith instead offered to buy the entire lot, mummies and manuscripts, from Chandler.

After completing his translation, Smith revealed *The Book of Abraham*. In this text, the patriarch Abraham recorded a revelation that he had received through use of the Urim and Thummim, special stones that God had given to facilitate such revelations. (Abraham 3:1) To him was revealed the secret of the stars, and one in particular very near to God's throne.

> And the Lord said unto me: These are the governing ones; and the name of the great one is Kolob, because it is near unto me, for I am the Lord thy God: I have set this one to govern all those which belong to the same order as that upon which thou standest. (Abraham 3:3)

The planet Kolob, according to *The Book of Abraham*, has a very different rate of revolution to the earth's. One day on Kolob is equal to 1,000 years on earth. The planet Kolob is set near to God's throne and reigns over the earth and all the planets of that order. The importance of the planet Kolob is expressed in the old Latter-Day Saint hymn, 'If You Could Hie to Kolob' by William W. Phelps.

> If you could hie to Kolob
> In the twinkling of an eye,
> And then continue onward
> With that same speed to fly,
> Do you think that you could ever,

UFO religion

> Through all eternity,
> Find out the generation
> Where Gods began to be?

The position of Latter-Day Saints on the topic of UFOs and life on other planets was elaborated by Kent Nielsen in his 1971 article 'People on Other Worlds,' and is featured on the official Latter-Day Saint website (Kent Nielsen, 'People on Other Worlds,' *New Era*, April 1971: 12). His claim is that the Latter-Day Saints possess the answers to the UFO mystery:

> One of the most exciting things for many Latter-day Saint students to learn is that the Church, through revelation from God (who – have you ever thought of it in this light? – is our contact from outer space), teaches some of the answers to these questions. And we've had the answers for quite some time.

The truth is that there are indeed people on other planets and those extraterrestrials have visited the earth and left important messages. As Nielsen says, 'When we put this all in perspective, it becomes very exciting: intelligent beings from a higher culture have visited earth frequently.'

Nielsen reminds his readers that Joseph Smith had taught that God himself was once a human like us, who dwelt on a planet like the earth. He was one of the created beings of his father. Through obedience to his father and redemption through a savior of that world he was given the power of godhood and began his own creation. In the same way, if we are obedient to God and faithful to the savior we shall be granted godhood and begin our own acts of creation upon other planets.

Thus in Latter-Day Saints doctrine we are told that investigations into ancient cultures, both American mound builder and Egyptian cultures in particular, reveal the truth of the extraterrestrial origin of life on earth and of civilization itself. Ancient documents, found long buried inside the mysterious American mounds or discovered by Egyptologists in the tomb of mummies, provide us with knowledge about life on other planets. Because of the historical setting of Mormonism's birth in the early eighteenth century there are, of course, no mentions of flying saucers or galactic congresses, for such are twentieth-century elements. Nevertheless,

Mormonism does share important features with contemporary UFO movements, not the least of which is the belief that ancient history, *properly interpreted*, can tell us many things about the nature of our universe and about life on other planets.

— Charles Fort —

Charles Fort was a collector of anomalies. A strong distrust of scientific orthodoxy combined with an unwavering interest in the weird led him to spend years in libraries collecting newspaper accounts that fell outside mainstream science and history. Much of today's tabloid newspaper fodder has its origins in the work of Fort: ghosts, crop circles, spontaneous combustion, ball lightning, strange animals or animals outside their normal habitats, and, of course, nocturnal lights are all a part of Fort's interesting anomalies – or is that anomalous interests? Fort wrote four books filled with his findings: *The Book of the Damned* in 1919, *New Lands* in 1923, *Lo!* in 1931, and *Wild Talents* in 1932. These books are strange compendiums of aberrant stories and facts that simply don't fit into any contemporary scientific theory. Fort doesn't necessarily think that all of his strange tales are true, but he argues that there are enough of them that it should call into question any claim of a science of everything.

For example, one type of phenomenon that Fort was interested in was the phenomenon of strange objects falling from the sky. He cataloged instances of fish, frogs, and even iron falling to the earth from the heavens. Perhaps one day there may even be reports of steel falling from the sky, he suggests. What shall we make of that? Perhaps above us are intelligences from other worlds who occasionally drop something overboard. When these unexplained objects drop in on us we are like the uneducated natives of a remote island who have no idea what it is that has washed up on our beach, or like a fish caught unaware by something from above.

> But what would a deep-sea fish learn even if a steel plate of a wrecked vessel above him should drop and bump him on the nose? Our submergence in a sea of conventionality of almost impenetrable density. Sometimes I'm a savage who has found

something on the beach of his island. Sometimes I'm a deep-sea fish with a sore nose. (Fort, 1974: 161–2)

The great mystery, Fort claims, is that if there are intelligences on other worlds and in the sky above us, why do they not contact us? Perhaps, he suggests, they have moral reasons for staying away, but if so we wonder that there are no immoral individuals among them. Maybe they simply are not interested us, but how can that be, considering human interest in such things as lowly as bugs and worms? Perhaps they worry about a collision, but can't they send rowboats ashore? The answer, says Fort, is obvious. They don't bother introducing themselves to us any more than we would bother introducing ourselves to our livestock. Perhaps they simply don't register us as being on the same plane of existence. He writes:

> Would we, if we could, educate and sophisticate pigs, geese, cattle? Would it be wise to establish diplomatic relation with the hen that now functions, satisfied with mere sense of achievement by way of compensation?
> I think we're property.
> I should say we belong to something:
> That once upon a time, this earth was No-man's Land, that other worlds explored and colonized here, and fought among themselves for possession, but that now it's owned by something:
> That something owns this earth – all others warned off.

And again,

> Pigs, geese, cattle.
> First find out they are owned.
> Then find out the whyness of it.
> I suspect that, after all, we're useful – that among contesting claimants, adjustment has occurred, or that something now has a legal right to us, by force, or by having paid out analogues of beads for us to former, more primitive, owners of us – all others warned off – that all this has been known, perhaps for ages, to certain ones upon this earth, a cult or order, members of which function like bellwethers to the rest of us, or as superior slaves or overseers, directing us in accordance with instructions received – from Somewhere else – in our mysterious usefulness. (Fort, 1974: 163)

Perhaps, before ownership of our planet was established, visitors from other worlds were more frequent. Maybe they,

> dropped here, hopped here, wafted, sailed, flown, motored – walked here, for all I know – been pulled here, been pushed; have come singly, have come in enormous numbers; have visited occasionally, have visited periodically for hunting, trading, replenishing harems, mining: have been unable to stay here, have established colonies here, have been lost here; far-advanced peoples, or things, and primitive peoples or whatever they were: white ones, black ones, yellow ones – (Fort, 1974: 164)

Maybe they established residence or taught the indigenous primitives some of their secrets. Maybe those same indigenous primitives worshiped these beings from space as gods. Perhaps the differences in the cultures of the earth can be understood as differences between the beings who founded them. Of the British, Fort says that he has sure knowledge of their ancestry.

> I have a very convincing datum that the ancient Britons were blue ones.
> Of course we are told by conventional anthropologists that they only painted themselves blue, but in our own advanced anthropology, they were veritable blue ones –
> Note of a blue child born in England.
> That's atavism. (Fort, 1974: 164)

According to Fort, there may have been many such parent worlds and colonies. The Super-Romanimus were the founders of Rome. (It's as good a story as Romulus and Remus, he reminds us.) The Israelites were established by the Super-Israelimus. And the British were founded by visitors from the planet Azuria, their descendants' color diluting over time, like blueing in a tub of water with the faucet running.

Fort's most explicit formulation of his claim that extraterrestrials had visited our planet in ancient times is found in his book *New Lands*. There he reported that he would one day publish information that would suggest that ancient mythology is actually a record of extraterrestrial visitations. The gods and demons of ancient myth might have in reality been 'beings and objects that visited this earth, not from a spiritual existence, but from outer space' (Fort, 1974:

419–20). It is reasonable to assume that, should beings from outer space appear before the primitive citizens of the earth, those space travelers would have been taken as gods and heroes. Without knowledge of astronomy these beings would have been said to have come from the sky above, rather than from the planets that must have assuredly been their home.

Charles Fort's books may not have been bestsellers in their day, but they have proved to be lasting in their influence. The idea of ancient astronauts, though he would not have called them that, visiting ancient earth and establishing races and civilizations is an idea that has struck a chord. Theme parks have been built around this idea. (More on that just a little later.) Exploring the same strange byways of history that Madame Blavatsky had followed, Fort finds the facts of the world, both ancient and modern, to be themselves alien. There is so much that cannot be placed under the schematics of any scientific theory. Alien facts call for alien explanations; that is what Fort provides. Beings from other worlds must have explored this world in the distant past, must have left their marks on everything they touched. Hence the alienness of those ancient days. Indeed, some of those alien beings may be here still, watching over us like farmers watching over their cattle, occasionally spotted out of the corner of our eyes. Hence the alienness we sometimes find in the morning newspaper or staring at us from a stranger's eyes.

— Desmond Leslie —

The 1953 book *Flying Saucers Have Landed* brought Adamski and the contactee movement international recognition. The book is properly lauded as the one of the most important publications of the flying saucer movement. Adamski, however, was responsible for only the last quarter of the book. The first two-thirds were written by Desmond Leslie. Apparently, when Adamski sent his brief monograph to the publisher they decided to team it with a recent submission by Leslie, thinking that the material was stronger together than apart. While Adamski's portion of the book is lauded as being extremely influential on the contactee movement, Leslie's contribution often goes unnoticed. To be fair, however, Leslie's portion of *Flying Sau-*

cers Have Landed may turn out to have been more influential than Adamski's, if not for the early contactee movement, then certainly for other segments of the saucer community. Leslie's accomplishment in *Flying Saucers Have Landed* was achieved through his synthesis of the ideas of Blavatsky, Fort, Shaver, and Keyhoe in such a way as to present the most coherent statement concerning the connection between the mysteries of ancient civilizations and UFOs that had yet been published in English. In just a few paragraphs in his foreword, Leslie manages to connect ancient mythology with the 1947 Kenneth Arnold flying saucer sightings, all the while expressing the spirit of Charles Fort. Leslie writes that it is

> to the lonely heretic who likes to walk alone down strange, untrodden paths; to him who believes all things are possible, particularly those things held by other men to be impossible; to him who leaves no stone unturned, and to him who gives a second chance to 'the stone rejected by the builders', that this book is dedicated.
> To these I offer some very curious stones for the turning; taking no responsibility whatsoever for anything they may find beneath. (Leslie and Adamski, 1953: 11)

Comparing contemporary flying saucer sightings with strange accounts from history, Desmond argues that the UFO phenomenon is not simply a recent fad, but a continuation of phenomena dating back into ancient times. Following Charles Fort, but with a bit more of a systematic approach, Leslie offers chronological lists of UFO sightings.

> 1619   Fluelen, Switzerland. Enormous long fiery object seen flying along a lake by Prefect Christopher Schere.
> 1661   Huge flaming things seen over Worcester, England.
> 1704   *January 8th*. Strange lights over England.
>   *November 4th*. Switzerland, Luminous cloud, moving at high velocity, disappeared behind the horizon. (Leslie and Adamski, 1953: 23)

Looking deeper into the past only reveals more mysterious references to flying saucers. Leslie finds many references to such craft in what he calls 'ancient Sanskrit descriptions.' Leslie claims that the *Samaranga Sutradhara* describes virmana, or flying craft, as made of lightweight materials and aerodynamically shaped. These craft could travel great distances, propelled by air. These craft were used for both peaceful activities and for warfare and may have operated by harnessing atomic power. According to Leslie, '[T]he ancients knew more than we imagine in that line; perhaps not nuclear fission, but some other aspects of atomic power which could be turned to peaceful or warlike uses with devastating results' (Leslie and Adamski, 1953: 92).

Leslie also claims that these craft were not simply used for terrestrial travel but for interstellar transport as well. Again citing the *Samar* as his sources, Leslie writes:

> Strictly and factually it makes the simple statement: '*By means of these machines, human beings can fly in the air and heavenly beings can come down to Earth.*'
>
> In other words, the ancients were quite accustomed to receiving men from other planets, even in those days. (Leslie and Adamski, 1953: 93)

Of special interest to Leslie was the mystery surrounding the construction of ancient monuments, monuments whose completion would be taxing upon the technology of modern civilization, much less the technology of the ancients. He cites the Irish Druidic stones of enormous weight whose origin, according to geologists, was in Egypt; the enormity of the stones used in the construction of the great pyramids; the huge monoliths of Easter Island; and the precision of measurements in ancient stonework. How could these great accomplishments have been carried out with the primitive technology of ancient civilizations? Once again, the logic of those who studied the American mounds in the nineteenth century, the logic of Joseph Smith, comes into play. The primitive peoples of the ancient past cannot have accomplished these feats. There is an alien quality about their monuments and buildings, about our inability to understand them. They must have alien origins, built under the guidance of beings from the stars who ruled the earth as gods and then mysteriously departed, only to make occasional appearances throughout history as strange lights in the night sky, or perhaps to make special contacts with chosen individuals.

The Egyptians wrote of the gods coming down from heaven in their shining vehicles bringing many gifts for men, gifts of food and gifts of teaching. The Red Indians have traditions that up till the coming of the white men, the elder brothers used to fly down in their circular shining ships to teach them and to help them in times of need. All the Celtic countries tell of the immortals coming down in flaming chariots from their shining places in the heavens to dwell on Earth amidst us. And it does not take much poetic imagination to call the bright planets 'shining palaces in the heavens', nor their spacecraft 'Flaming Chariots'. (Leslie and Adamski, 1953: 169)

— Erich von Däniken —

While Leslie's contribution to *Flying Saucers Have Landed* clearly helped to foster among saucerians the idea that extraterrestrials had visited the earth in the ancient past, it was Erich von Däniken who first introduced ancient astronauts to popular culture. His most popular work, *Chariots of the Gods,* and the film based on the book were veritable pop culture sensations. Like Leslie before him, and obviously influenced by him, von Däniken combined a healthy dose of Theosophy and Forteana with contemporary UFO sightings to offer a solution to what he called the 'Unsolved Mysteries of the Past.' Looking beyond ancient writings to explore ancient artwork and iconography, von Däniken provided not just translations of ancient texts but also photographs of ancient drawings depicting flying saucers and spacemen.

For example, in Peru near the ancient city of Nazca, are lines that have been laid out across the plain. Von Däniken says that archeologists have described these lines as ancient roads, as an ancient calendar, or as containing some religious significance. His own investigations, however, revealed something very different and show us a lot about von Däniken's methodology.

Flying above the plains of Nazca, von Däniken claims that he was immediately struck by the answer to the mystery. The clear impression that the lines of Nazca make is of an airfield! This theory is, of course, immediately rejected by mainstream archeologists, who assume without questioning that the ancient people of Nazca could not have had any use for an airstrip. It is this and similar assumptions on the part of archeologists that make them blind to the truth; they miss the obvious. Enormous markings on the ground that can only be appreciated from above are clearly meant to be seen from the air! Combine this with other huge drawings scratched into the earth and into mountainsides and only one conclusion is reasonable, says von Däniken. The Nazca civilization must have believed that these images were being observed from above.

Von Däniken finds evidence of extraterrestrial visitors in the Bible as well. The story of the destruction of Sodom and Gomorrah, for example, makes little sense when taken as an account of angels rushing to save Lot from the wrath of God. Why would God simply not delay the destruction until Lot was safely removed? Why was God seemingly bound to a timetable? These problems disappear when we take the account of angelic visitors as an account of extra-terrestrials come to earth. This is how von Däniken theorizes the actual events might have taken place:

> Let us imagine for a moment that Sodom and Gomorrah were destroyed according to plan, i.e., deliberately, by a nuclear explosion. Perhaps – let us speculate a little further – the 'angels' simply wanted to destroy some dangerous fissionable material and at the same time to make sure of wiping out a human brood they found unpleasant. The time for the destruction was fixed. Those who were to escape it – such as the Lot family – had to stay a few miles from the center of the explosion in the mountains, for the rock faces would naturally absorb the dangerous rays. And – we all know the story – Lot's wife turned around and looked straight at the atomic sun. Nowadays no one is surprised that she fell dead on the spot. 'Then the Lord rained upon Sodom and Gomorrah brimstone and fire.' (von Däniken, 1968: 53–4)

In these two examples, the Lines of Nazca and the story of Sodom and Gomorrah, von Däniken's methodology is clearly displayed. The best way to interpret ancient texts and ancient monuments is to look for similarities with things in the modern world. Lines in a desert must be a landing strip; fire from heaven must be an atomic bomb. Of course, once we assume the existence of landing strips and atomic bombs in antiquity we must then provide an explanation for these things, since they would have clearly been beyond the capabilities of the ancient humans. Could the answer be that the ancient world was visited by extraterrestrials?

Von Däniken describes his thesis as follows:

> Dim, as yet undefinable ages ago an unknown spaceship discovered our planet. The crew of the spaceship soon found out that the earth had all the prerequisites for intelligent life to develop. Obviously the 'man' of those times was no *homo sapiens* but something rather different. The spacemen artificially fertilized some female members of this species, put them into a deep sleep, so ancient legends say, and departed. Thousands of years later the space travelers returned and found scattered specimens of the genus *homo sapiens*. They repeated their breeding experiment several times until finally they produced a creature intelligent enough to have the rules of society imparted to it. The people of that age were still barbaric. Because there was a danger that they might retrogress and mate with animals again, the space travelers destroyed the unsuccessful specimens or took them with them to settle them on other continents. The first communities and the first skills came into being; rock faces and cave walls were painted, pottery was discovered, and the first attempts at architecture were made.
>
> These first men had tremendous respect for the space travelers. Because they came from somewhere absolutely unknown and then returned there again, they were the 'gods' to them. For some mysterious reason the 'gods' were interested in passing on their intelligence. They took care of the creatures they bred; they wanted to protect them from corruption and preserve them from evil. They wanted to ensure that their community developed constructively. They wiped out the freaks and saw to it that the remainder received the basic requirements for a society capable of development. (von Däniken, 1968: 70)

In support of this thesis von Däniken piles on example after example of ancient story or ancient monument that seems to fit into his scheme. Eskimos talked about metal birds bringing the first people to their northern land. The ancient Mayans knew that the earth was round. The pre-Incan peoples believed that the stars were inhabited by 'gods'. Some of these 'gods' – shades of Billy Meier – were said to have visited the earth from the Pleiades. An inscription discovered on an Egyptian pyramid reads 'Thou art he who directs the sun ship of millions of years.' Elijah, prophet of the Hebrew Bible, is taken into the sky in a fiery chariot. Time and again modern scholars dismiss such as mythology because they cannot, or will not, believe that the ancients were giving a factual account of their experiences. Perhaps they are bothered that the stories call them iron birds and flaming chariots rather than spaceships or rockets. But surely, von Däniken argues, they were using the categories of their day to describe these extraordinary sights. He gives an example.

> A helicopter lands in the African bush for the first time. None of the natives has ever seen such a machine. The helicopter lands in a clearing with a sinister clatter; pilots in battle dress, with crash helmets and machine guns, jump out of it. The savage in his loin cloth stands stupefied and uncomprehending in the presence of this thing that has come down from heaven and the unknown 'gods' who came with it. After a time the helicopter takes off again and disappears into the sky.
> Once he is alone again, the savage has to work out and interpret this apparition. He will tell others who are not present what he saw: a bird, a heavenly vehicle, that made a terrible noise and stank, and white-skinned creatures carrying weapons that spat fire. The miraculous visit is fixed and handed down for all time. When the father tells his son, the heavenly bird obviously does not get any smaller, and the creatures that get out of it become weirder, stronger, and more imposing. (von Däniken, 1968: 79)

Von Däniken's theory of ancient astronauts is an attempt to explain the origins of ancient culture and the origins of religion. Though remaining vague about the actual events of the ancient past, he is convinced that human culture was affected by extraterrestrial visitors and that those visitors are the source of the stories of the gods. His approach places ancient cultures in both a positive and a negative light. He claims that we should not treat ancient people like children, that we should take their words and their records as actual descriptions of what occurred. His argument is that appreciation for what they recorded in their texts and in their artwork is paramount. We must begin there.

> Certain things cannot be made up. I should not be ransacking our prehistory for space travelers and heavenly aircraft if accounts of such apparitions appeared in only two or three ancient books. But when in fact nearly all the texts of the primitive peoples all over the globe tell the same story, I feel I must try to explain the objective thrust concealed in their pages. (von Däniken, 1968: 79)

At the same time, he remains driven by that old assumption that ancient people simply could not have accomplished the great things we know that they did accomplish without help from a more advanced source.

Von Däniken's latest venture was an attempt to mainstream his particular brand of alternative history by incorporating the themes of his theory into a theme park. In 2002, von Däniken opened Mystery Park in Interlaken, Switzerland. According to von Däniken, he plans for the park to become a center for research concerning the great mysteries of the world and for what von Däniken now calls Paleo-SETI, or the search for evidence of ancient astronauts.

Mystery Park is made up of seven 'theme worlds' built around a central circle. The central sphere is open to the public and houses the offices of von Däniken himself. The theme worlds include 'The Orient', which explores the mystery of the pyramids; 'The Vimanas', which explores the flying craft of ancient India; 'The Maya', an exploration of the ancient Mayan calendar, which ends in the year 2012; 'The MegaStones', which ponders the mystery of Stonehenge and other ancient relics and wonders if they could have been time machines; 'Contact', an examination of the evidence for extraterrestrial contact with early humans; 'Nazca', which explores the meaning of the drawings on the Nazca plain; and 'Challenge', devoted to a presentation of facts about SETI, the international Search for Extraterrestrial Intelligence.

— Zecharia Sitchin —

Probably the most important proponent of the Ancient Astronaut theory today, despite von Däniken's Mystery Park, is Zecharia Sitchin. While accepting the basic thesis put forward by Leslie and von Däniken that the earth was visited by extraterrestrials in the distant past, that these extraterrestrials were responsible for the beginnings of civilization and the construction of ancient wonders, and that these extraterrestrials were treated as gods by the people of earth, Sitchin offers a far more detailed analysis of the events of that ancient contact with extraterrestrials. His claims are elaborated in great detail in his *Earth Chronicles* series of books, including the bestseller *The 12th Planet*. A more succinct account can be found in *Genesis Revisited* (1990).

Sitchin's interpretation of ancient Sumerian documents, documents that he claims only he can correctly understand, follows von Däniken in treating the mythological stories of the gods as accurate portrayals of actual history. The Sumerian culture, according to Sitchin, suddenly appeared some six thousand years ago, a civilization without precedent emerging suddenly and without explanation. This civilization not only employed the wheel, written language, civil law, and art, but also had a very advanced understanding of astronomy. Amazingly, however, their picture of the solar system was very different to ours. One difference in the Sumerian understanding of astronomy had to do with the planet Pluto (no, it wasn't just discovered in the twentieth century, but was know by the ancients before it was forgotten). For the Sumerians, Pluto was understood to have been a moon of the planet Saturn that was freed from that orbit to take its place among the planets. The second major difference in Sumerian astronomy and modern science is that the Sumerian version of the solar system included a large planet between Mars and Jupiter. This is the twelfth planet, if one counts the sun and moon as planets in the way that the Sumerians did. This planet was called NIBIRU by the Sumerians. The planet of NIBIRU, according to Sumerian astronomy, passes between Mars and Jupiter every 3,600 years. From NIBIRU, extraterrestrials known as the Anunnaki came to this planet. The Anunnaki (sometimes called the Nefilim) first came to earth some 445,000 years ago by Sitchin's reckoning and at that time were a very advanced civilization. They made return visits every time their planet passed near enough to the earth.

What motive brought them to our planet time and time again? Sitchin finds an answer in the Sumerian texts for this question as well. The planet NIBIRU faced an ecological crisis and it was critically important that the Anunnaki protect their atmosphere. A solution to their problem was to scatter gold particles above the atmosphere to act as a protective shield. (Windows on American spacecraft are coated with gold to protect against radiation, Sitchin informs the reader in *Genesis Revisited* (1990: 19)) The Anunnaki discovered that the seventh planet – earth if counting from the outer solar system toward the sun – was rich in gold. Beginning with a fruitless attempt to collect gold from the Persian Gulf, the Anunnaki then began to mine for gold in southern Africa.

Around 300,000 years ago a critical event took place: tired of being forced to mine gold on the primitive seventh planet, the Anunnaki who had been assigned to the mines revolted. Enki (a sort of cross between Dr. McCoy and Mr. Spock for all you nerds out there), the chief scientist and chief medical officer of the mining colony, manipulated the genetic code of one species of earth animal and produced creatures that could carry out the mining work in place of the unhappy Anunnaki. By crossing the genes of the Annunnaki with *Homo erectus*, *Homo sapiens* were born.

The relationship between the Anunnaki and humans was one of god and servant, but some good did come from the relationship. Human culture, including science, art, and religion, was carefully cultivated by the Anunnaki lords. Over time, the declining need for gold and the nuances of NIBIRU politics (described in great detail by Sitchin in his *Earth Chronicles* series) resulted in the abandonment of the earth mission. For centuries the Anunnaki have not been among us. However, Sitchin warns, the time for NIBIRU's passing draws near again. While Sitchin has remained vague about the exact date of NIBIRU's appearance, many assume that it will occur in the year 2012, the last year of the Mayan calendar.

Sitchin suggests that we may not have been left quite as alone as we have been led to believe. While the Anunnaki seem to have certainly left the planet, is it not possible that they have the capability to monitor our progress and development? Of course the idea of spaceships traveling the great distance between earth and NIBIRU at the point of their greatest separation is a stretch of the imagination, but is it not possible that they established a base on the planet Mars, from where exploratory missions could be made quite easily? Such a Mars base would offer solutions to two mysteries of the day. First, it would explain the UFO phenomenon and the claims of abductees. Flying saucers are real. Just as popular culture has long believed, they come from Mars, but they are not Martians, they are Anunnaki. Second, it would explain the mystery of the monuments and structures discovered on Mars, all of which have been dismissed by official science.

UFO religion

Sitchin's theories have not gone unchallenged, as one might imagine. For our purposes, however, we will ignore those challenges offered by mainstream astronomers, historians, archeologists, and anthropologists. Criticism from these quarters must take a back seat to charges that Sitchin is in league with a race of reptilian extraterrestrials. Leading this charge against Sitchin is David Icke.

Icke, for example rejects Sitchin's NIBIRU theory because an orbit like the one postulated for the twelfth planet would be erratic and difficult to sustain. He does accept the main parts of Sitchin's theory concerning the Anunnaki, though he suspects that gold was not the only reason for their mission to earth, if it was a reason at all. Icke adds that catastrophic events on the planet from 11,000 to 1,500 BCE ended the earlier golden age of humanity and caused many extraterrestrials to flee the planet or to find shelter underground. The survivors of the difficult days included both humans and extraterrestrials. Some of the extraterrestrials shared their knowledge with the surviving humans in order to help them rebuild their civilizations. Other extraterrestrials refused to do so. (Shades of Shaver!) The struggle between the two camps of ETs has been expressed through the manipulation of human history. Icke claims that the Anunnaki are a race of reptilian, or reptoid, aliens. He also believes that other races of extraterrestrials may have lived on earth in antiquity and competed and warred with the reptoid Anunnaki.

Connecting the reptoid Anunnaki to legends of underground races, Icke claims that a Hopi Indian legend tells of caverns and catacombs underneath Los Angeles, California. This system of tunnels was located in the 1930s and is today used for secret Freemasonic rituals, illustrating the connection between the malevolent reptoids and secret societies that rule the world. From there, Icke's theories only get weirder. At this point I must let him speak for himself.

> Summarizing all the research I have read, the people I have met, and the accounts of those who claim to have experienced these reptile humanoids or reptilians, the following appears to be the case. There are many sub and crossbreed races of the reptilians. Their elite is known by UFO researchers as the Draco. These are the 'big boys' in every sense and they are usually between seven and twelve feet tall. They have wings which are flaps of skin sup-

ported by long ribs. The wings can be folded back against the body and they are the origin of the term 'winged serpent'.

They are also the origin of the term 'fallen angels' and the winged gargoyles are symbolic of these Draco. The cape worn by Count Dracula is symbolic of these wings and the character of Dracula in the Bram Stoker stories is said to be a fallen angel. The winged Draco are also known as the Dragon Race and some of the ancient gods were described and depicted as birdmen. This could be one of the origins of the Phoenix and eagle in Brotherhood symbolism, as well as the more esoteric meanings. The biblical Satan is depicted as a reptilian, too. (Icke, 1999: 37)

Not only are the Anunnaki reptoids the source of the vampire legends, they are also the source of the stories of the blood-sucking Chupacabara.

It is possible, we are told, that the Anunnaki cross-bred with a species of white Martian before coming to earth and may indeed work in tandem with the race of white beings (Tall Whites?). Indeed, the whites and grays are thought to work with the reptoids in the program of cross-breeding that has allowed the reptoids to pass as human and which has created a reptoid bloodline within the human race, members of which work for the reptoid cause. This cross-breeding has been crucial to the success of the reptoids in their bid to control our planet.

The network of reptoids passing as human and of humans of the reptoid lineage has been responsible for nearly every major event in history. The reptoid alliance is responsible for the deaths of Princess Diana and John Kennedy. The royal family of England and all leaders of the major nations of the world are part of this vast conspiracy. It matters not which American political party one votes for. It is guaranteed that whoever is elected will be under the influence of reptoids in one form or another. The Bush family is a part of the reptoid bloodline. Bill Clinton is not, but was under the command of the reptoids. Hillary Clinton is a member of the reptoid family. Al Gore is known to be addicted to human blood and has been seen to shapeshift in public into his true reptoid form.

◆ ◆ ◆

UFO religion

I really cannot imagine a form of life in which one would mistake a National Guard exercise for the End of the World. Someone who would make that mistake is alien to me. My grandmother could not comprehend the war machines that swooped down upon her farm like fallen angels. They were beyond her experience, alien to her way of life. They must have been the work of God. I face her as the unknown past. She faced the war machines as the unknown future. The future strains to understand the past; the past strains to comprehend the future. The space between the two is an alien landscape.

The unknown past demands that we seek out its mysteries. The skeletal remains of past civilizations wait for us to put flesh on their bones, to clothe them with stories and ideas and images. They are not content to be left for dead. We are their Dr. Frankenstein, Jesus to their Lazarus. Yet they seem so different from us, like the bones, not of humans, but of some long-extinct species that we hardly recognize. We piece them together, bone by bone, and stand in wonder before what we have discovered. They are alien. Not much different to the bodies recovered at Roswell, or Aztec, or Aurora; their origin cannot be of the earth, not the earth that we know. They must come from elsewhere, from the stars. Assuredly if they could see us even as dimly as we see them the reaction would be the same.

It seems that proponents of the Ancient Astronaut theory, and Joseph Smith – for whom such a term is admittedly anachronistic – are responding to this problem. Because the past is so far removed, because the wonders of the ancients seem too much for us to understand, it is easy to make them into aliens, easy to find their source beyond the stars. Likewise the future, uncertain and unsure, more alien than the past: it is not as glimpsed through robot rover eyes, but an unknown planet yet to be explored. If we look, as Fort taught us to do, we may see signs and wonders today as well, mistaken for illusions or miracles, they may be glimpses of the future, the alien, that serve to remind us that our understanding may be no greater than our ancestors', that we may make mistakes as important as my grandmother's, as important as the ancients' when they mistook visitors from space to be gods among them. There is a wonder here, a wonder about the past and a wonder about the future.

Icke and his like are another matter. Here there is not wonder before antiquity or futurity. Here there is only alienation, alienation from society and from politics and from the ways that we live together as people. Here, the alien does not engender wonder, only fear. There are monsters in our midst, shapeshifting reptoids who drink human blood and rule the world. Resistance is futile; hope is unreasonable. You can trust no one, believe in no one. Ickes's fear is directed toward those in power and in that it is more understandable and less troublesome than the fear that some express, like those who fear the other kind of aliens, people with dark skin and strange accents who have invaded our world and threaten our jobs. For some, aliens are the aliens. For Icke, it is just the opposite. The aliens are those who seem to be most in league with our world. I suppose that is the real crux of the problem: the world itself is alien, is alienated, from Icke and those like him. Furthermore, his elucidation of that alienation makes me fear him, makes him alien to me in ways that he was not before. It is the trouble with tribbles. Alienation breeds alienation, aliens breed aliens. No, it is not the trouble with tribbles, but 'The Invasion of the Body Snatchers' and now we find that we need someone to save us from ourselves.

8

Gods from Outer Space

A Couch Tom Cruise Won't Jump On
Actor Lambastes Psychiatry on 'Today'
(*Washington Post*, Saturday, June 25, 2005)

Tom Cruise Confronts Rumors About Silent Birth
(ABC News, April 13, 2006)

US Government Probes Cloning Claim
(BBC News, Sunday, December 29, 2002)

Who Are the Raelians?
The news of a second 'cloned' baby has piqued further interest in
this tiny, controversial sect. One member speaks out
(Time.com, January 4, 2003)

Religious Rift Brews in Rural Georgia
Group claims harassment; county wants building code enforced
(CNN.com, June 29, 1999)

Sect Leader Found Guilty of Child Molestation
(CNN.com, January 23, 2004)

— Scientology —

L. Ron Hubbard wrote many science fiction stories for the pulp magazines in the 1930s and developed a strong following for his
particular brand of space opera. He would not receive fame, however, until the publication in 1950 of his non-fiction book *Dianetics:
The Modern Science of Mental Health*. Dianetics did not mark a break

with his pulp fiction past, however, as his friend and sci-fi editor John W. Campbell promoted Hubbard's book in the pages of *Astounding Science Fiction*. The science of mental health, as elaborated by Hubbard in this book, consisted of a particular form of therapy in which two people participate in a session of questions and answers in the exploration of painful memories, a practice Hubbard called auditing. Auditing, according to Hubbard, could reduce stress, increase intelligence, and cure illnesses. Later Hubbard would update and expand his theory of Dianetics under the name Scientology.

Like Dianetics, Scientology has at its core the practice of auditing, in which individuals may confront painful memories from this life, and from other past lives, in an attempt to free their soul from the many burdens acquired through time. The audits are usually performed with an E-meter, an electronic device that helps the auditor determine the progress of the practitioner. Through auditing, an individual may progress through multiple levels of knowledge, awareness, and spiritual maturity until freedom is achieved. In the vocabulary of Scientology, a preclear participates in auditing so as to become free of engrams and implants acquired throughout countless past lives, on this planet and others, and in order to reach the state of Clear and to become an Operating Thetan. Unlike most other such groups, who are more than happy to share their teachings for free, Scientologists charge fees for the auditing sessions and for access to many of their doctrines.

Several elements of Scientology have received attention from the press in recent years. For example, Hubbard taught that the birth of a child should be accompanied by as much quiet as possible because the experience is traumatic for the baby. Hearing words that were once spoken in the delivery room again later in life might cause adults to relive the trauma of birth. Thus silent birthing is directly related to the central tenets of Scientology. Problems in the human mind, including mental problems that express themselves as physical problems, are the result of traumas and negative experiences. The goal of Scientology is not only to assist individuals through auditing to resolve past traumas but also to assist individuals in the avoidance of new traumas.

UFO religion

Another element of Scientology that has received some attention is the movement's opposition to psychiatry. Hubbard completely rejected the theory that mental disorders may have physical causes and in doing so rejected the practice of psychiatry. His criticism of the field seemed to run deeper than a mere difference of opinion about the causes of mental disorders, however. Hubbard believed that one of the greatest missions of Scientology was to actively oppose psychiatry and to offer auditing as an alternative.

Perhaps the most tantalizing thing about Scientology, however, is what we don't know. A large portion of Scientology's teachings are meant only for the ears of initiates. Through the process of auditing, preclears pass through eight Operating Thetan stages and at each stage more information is granted to them. By all accounts the most secretive level is called Operating Thetan Level III, or OT III. Hubbard claimed to have arrived at the truths contained in OT III through his own auditing process and consequent recovered memories. OT III claims to reveal central events in human history, and because of the importance of these teachings Scientologists are not exposed to the material until it is certain that they are prepared to receive the truth contained therein. Hubbard is said to have acquired the knowledge in 1967, on a trip to North Africa, and claimed that he was lucky to have lived through the experience.

According to OT III, thetans are immortal souls who have existed from eternity as separate and independent entities. Each human being is, in essence, such a thetan. Upon the origination of the material universe thetans became trapped within material substance. This entrapment, or implanting, is the result of a delusion that causes thetans to forget their own nature and to believe that their existence is dependent upon material reality. The goal of Scientology, then, is to free thetans from this imprisonment, thus creating Operating, or free, Thetans once again.

There are complexities to this doctrine, however. According to the secret materials, many millions of years ago seventy-six planets in our galaxy, united as the Galactic Federation, were ruled over by the evil Xenu. As the planets under his dominion became overcrowded, Xenu gathered a large contingent of his population and had them transported by spaceships to the planet Teegeeack, a planet known to us as earth. Xenu was not simply relocating them to earth, however, for once on earth they, along with a representative group of the earth's population, were dropped from the spaceships into the mouths of active volcanoes. As if this were not enough they were then completely vaporized by hydrogen bombs. The scattered souls, or thetans, of those murdered by Xenu were trapped in electronic devices and implanted with various types of misleading circuits and false memories. These implanted delusions included the notion of religion, a notion that served to further delude thetans concerning their true nature.

Over time, many of these thetans became attached to human bodies, as what are called 'body thetans', thus burdening earth humans with all of the pain and trauma of the attached body thetans. Unfortunately, the body thetans often attach to bodies in clumps, meaning that any one human body may be covered with a large number of thetans, some intertwined in difficult-to-unravel clumps.

As for Xenu, he was later captured, after a six-year battle, by officers loyal to the people of the federation. He was locked away in a mountain prison where he remains to this day. The only way to truly defeat him, however, is to engage in the long process of auditing until one is able to remove the body thetans that have become attached as well as the false implants that keep the truth hidden from us. Some Scientologists claim that the number of body thetans attached to them number in the millions. These body thetans must be dealt with one at a time, through the auditing process, even though many of them have been crushed together as clusters by shared traumatic experiences. In addition to freeing themselves from the body thetans, preclears must also find a way to free themselves from the implanted delusions; in essence to become aware of their true nature as eternal, immaterial spirits. To complicate matters, Hubbard taught that what he called the 'R6' implant was booby-trapped, so that attempted removal could cause the individual to be stricken with pneumonia.

If this sounds strange to us it is because we are not yet prepared to hear the truth. It is only after progressing, by auditing, through the first two Operating Thetan levels that one is free enough of implanted delusions to be able to accept the truth of the story of Xenu and the body thetans. Scientologists have struggled to maintain the secrets of OT III, but with the pervasiveness of the internet and the willingness of ex-Scientologists to tell what they know, it has become increasingly difficult to keep their secrets. Scientology is unique within the UFO culture because of this secretiveness, as well as because of the capitalist format under which they operate. Scientology is also difficult to categorize. While it bears strong similarities to the Ashtar Command or the Aetherius Society, its emphasis upon the Xenu event as the central message of the group seems to place them within the ancient astronaut tradition. Either way, Scientology is perhaps most different from other UFO groups in their attempt to keep all of the space opera stuff under wraps. They really would have preferred the rest of us not to know about Xenu and the galactic federation. Alas, such secrets are hard to keep.

— Raelians —

The Raelian movement is more directly connected to ancient astronaut theories and to the work of von Däniken than is Scientology. It also shares many elements with the contactee movements. According to its founder, Claude Vorilhon, his first ET encounter occurred in 1973. On his way to work Vorilhon felt strangely compelled to drive past his office and to a volcano near Auvergne, France. At the volcano Vorilhon made his way on foot toward the center of the crater. After exploring the crater and returning to his car, he saw a strange red light dropping from the sky. As it drew near and was directly above him, Vorilhon could discern the craft's saucer shape. This is how he describes it:

> The object continued to descend, without the slightest noise until it stopped and hovered motionless about two meters above the ground. I was petrified and remained absolutely still. I was not afraid, but rather filled with joy to be living through such a great moment. I bitterly regretted not having brought my camera with me.
>
> Then the incredible happened. A trap door opened beneath the machine and a kind of stairway unfolded to the ground. I

realized that some living being was about to appear, and I wondered what it was going to look like.

First two feet appeared then two legs, which reassured me a little, since apparently I was about to meet a man. In the event, what at first I took to be a child came down the stairway and walked straight towards me.

I could see then this was certainly no child even though the figure was only about four feet tall. His eyes were slightly almond shaped, his hair was black and long, and he had a small black beard. I still had not moved, and he stopped about ten meters away from me.

He wore some sort of green one-piece suit, which covered his entire body, and although his head seemed to be exposed, I could see around it a strange sort of halo. It was not really a halo but the air about his face shone slightly and shimmered. It looked like an invisible shield, like a bubble, so fine that you could barely see it. His skin was white with a slightly greenish tinge, a bit like someone with liver trouble.

The being informed Vorilhon that he had been chosen for a special mission.

Listen to me carefully. You will tell human beings about this meeting but you will tell them the truth about what they are, and about what we are. Judging from their reactions we will know if we can show ourselves freely and officially. Wait until you know everything before you start speaking publicly. Then you will be able to defend yourself properly against those people who will not believe you and you will be able to bring them incontestable proof. You will write down everything I tell you and publish the writings as a book. (Rael, 2005: 5 and 7–8)

Reminiscent of the Apostle Paul in Christian scriptures, Vorilhon was given a new name by his alien contact, the name Rael. The truth about humanity that Rael was called to share is that humans were created by beings from another planet known as the Elohim. The term Elohim appears in the Judeo-Christian Bible and is mistranslated as 'God'. It literally means 'those who come from the sky'. Thus, and by now this should be familiar, the Biblical stories that have been interpreted as stories about God and his angels are in reality stories about the alien Elohim. As with von Däniken and Sitchin, the stories of the gods are actually stories of the activities of extraterrestrials.

UFO religion

At Rael's next meeting with his little green friend the details of the creation of human beings were revealed.

> A very long time ago on our distant planet, we had reached a level of technical and scientific knowledge, comparable to that which you will soon reach. Our scientists had started to create primitive, embryonic forms of life, namely living cells in test tubes. Everyone was thrilled by this.
> The scientists perfected their techniques and began creating bizarre little animals but the government, under pressure from public opinion, ordered the scientists to stop their experiments for fear they would create monsters, which would become dangerous to society. In fact one of these animals had broken loose and killed several people. (Rael, 2005: 10)

Taking their experiments to another planet so as to be free of government regulation, the Elohim scientists began work on planet earth. After much work they created flora and fauna to cover the planet. It was then that they decided to move on to bigger and better things.

> It was at that time that the most skillful among us wanted to create an artificial human being like ourselves. Each team set to work, and very soon we were able to compare our creations. But on our home planet people were outraged when they heard that we were making 'test tube children' who might come to threaten their world. They feared that these new human beings could become a danger if their mental capacities or powers turned out to be superior to those of their creators. So we had to leave the new humans to live in a very primitive way without letting them know anything scientific, and we mystified our actions. (Rael, 2005: 15)

As with Sitchin, Rael's story of the beginnings of humanity is quite complex. He too translates the stories found in the Hebrew Bible into accounts of the intrigues and dramas of the Elohim and their creations.

Crucial for an understanding of Rael's message is knowledge that the present age is the age of apocalypse, a time when humans are finally advanced enough to accept the truth about their beginnings. The age of apocalypse will mark the return of the Elohim to the earth. In preparation for this Rael was asked to build an embassy to receive the Elohim upon their return, which will only occur when humans have achieved world peace, a goal that can only be reached as love is spread around the world and the truth of Rael's message is accepted and put into practice.

Like many UFO groups, Raelian metaphysics are quite developed. The planet earth is believed to be an atom in the body of an extremely large being. This being is part of a planet that is one atom of an even bigger being, and so on. These infinite levels of life also extend in the other direction. The atoms of our bodies are planets that contain living beings whose atoms are the planet homes of even smaller beings. The Raelians believe that God is without material substance, but that human immortality is a purely material concept. Souls do not live on beyond the life of the body. Rather, immortality is achieved through the revitalization of human bodies through genetic cloning. Immortality, therefore, is only achieved through a complex, and purely scientific, process. Rael has carefully indicated what the process will be like.

First, a genetically identical human clone must be created. The Raelians believe that such a thing is possible with present technology. As a matter of fact they recently claimed to have sponsored the cloning of such a human being through the scientific arm of their organization, Clonaid, but they were never able to provide any proof of their success. Second, the clone must be made to mature rapidly. Rael believes that in the near future scientists will be able to accomplish this, perhaps through advancements in nanotechnology. Third, the memory and personality of the human being must be transferred to the mature clone. This process, though difficult and still not a reality in terms of scientific technology, is the only way to immortality. For all of those unfortunate individuals who die before the technology is developed there is still hope. The DNA and memories of deceased humans, at least those who have died in the last ten centuries or so, are maintained on file by the Elohim. Thus, upon their return, there will be a scientific resurrection of the dead as the Elohim assist human scientists in creating clones and implanting memories.

Rael's materialism is also found in his ethical teachings. The Raelians believe that human behavior should not be guided by misleading 'spiritual laws' but rather by a utilitarian quest for the largest amount of pleasures for the largest number of people. For the Raelians this often involves the practice of unrestricted sexual behavior.

> Each one of our organs was created by our parents, the Elohim, so that we might use it feeling not shame, but happiness at using something for which it was designed. If the act of using one of our organs brings pleasure, it means that our creators wish us to have that pleasure.
> Every individual is a garden that should not be left uncultivated. A life without pleasure is an uncultivated garden. Pleasure is the fertilizer that opens up the mind. (Rael, 2005: 187)

In illustration, one of the Raelians' current humanitarian projects is the Clitoraid program which encourages people to 'Adopt a Clitoris'. Responding to the tragedy that is female circumcision the Raelians believe that a solution to the problem is possible through medical practices designed to rebuild a woman's clitoris. Likewise, in response to a movement known as JC's Girls – comprised of women formerly involved in the sex industry who attempt to lead other women to faith in Jesus and away from their profession – Raelians have encouraged the development of Rael's Girls, an organization of women who wish to help women in the sex industry, and customers of the sex industry, to understand that the best way to achieve satisfaction in life is through physical pleasure. Rael's Girls want women in the sex industry to do their work free of guilt and to achieve as much pleasure for themselves as possible.

Despite the Raelians' sexual ethics and materialistic world view they have found themselves on the same side as fundamentalist Christians when it comes to the rejection of Darwinism in favor of the intelligent design of human beings. Rael and his followers are as opposed to evolution as the explanation for human origins as are the conservative Christians they are otherwise in disagreement with. Of course, the Raelian version of creation is very different from the Judeo-Christian one. It even allows for the fact that primates and humans are closely related, as was revealed to Rael.

> Your scientists who have elaborated theories of evolution are not completely wrong in saying that humanity is descended from the monkey, and the monkey from the fish, and so on. In reality, the

first living organism created on Earth was unicellular, which then gave rise to more complex life forms.

But this did not happen by chance! When we came to Earth to create life, we started by making very simple creations and then improved our techniques of environmental adaptation. This enabled us to make in turn fish, amphibians, mammals, birds, primates, and finally – man himself, who is just an improved model of the monkey to which we added what makes us essentially human. (Rael, 2005: 92)

Freely mixing elements found in both contactee stories and ancient astronaut theories, Rael's teachings make explicit an element that is only hinted at in the others, an abiding faith in science. I suppose that such a faith is common to much of UFO culture. After all, to believe in flying saucers, even if you aren't concerned with the nuts and bolts, is to have faith in the ability of science. It is science and technology that allow the visitors from Mars, Venus, Saturn, Clarion, NIBIRU and the Pleiades to travel those great distances across the void of space, sometimes to warn us, sometimes to guide us, sometimes just to return a borrowed camera. Rael makes that faith a central component of his story. It is through the efforts of science and technology that all life on earth came to be. It is through science that humans shall gain eternal life.

Of course, Rael's faith in science is terribly naive. There is seemingly no recognition of the complexities involved in such issues as human cloning, no recognition that technology can be used for evil rather than good. The Raelians are certainly not a doomsday cult. This is the age of the apocalypse, but apocalypse here has it original meaning. The apocalypse does not signify the judgment and wrath of God; it means rather an unveiling, a revealing of the truth. In Rael's vision the future will be as those science fiction stories told us it would be. Technology will solve all our problems and grant us eternal life. I cannot help but think that their faith is misplaced, that they have failed to learn the lessons of history, failed to learn that technology is usually driven by the needs of the military rather than the needs of humanity. Here, an alternative history seems to allow for an alternative future, a future that I cannot embrace, though a part of me wishes I could.

— The Nuwaubian Nation of Moors —

The homeland of the Yamassee Indian Tribe is located in central Georgia, in the southern United States. This is only extraordinary because the Yamassee tribe is composed almost entirely of African Americans. While their twentieth-century settlement is designed to be reminiscent of the tribe's traditional buildings and architecture, the style is definitely not Native American, but rather ancient Egyptian. Pyramids and an obelisk rising from the farmlands of Georgia are sure signs that something strange is going on here.

Patricia J. Mays described the settlement in a report for the Associated Press.

> Eatonton, Ga. – A huge white pylon with paintings of Egyptian pharaohs juts out of the red clay of middle Georgia, conspicuous among the miles of pines, dairy farms and mobile homes. Within the gated commune behind the pylon, members of the United Nuwaubian Nation of Moors hustle around replicas of Egyptian pyramids and a Sphinx. . . . This 476-acre rural Putnam County site [is] what the Nuwaubians refer to as the 'Little Egypt of the West,' their safe-haven away from the problems that plague the outside world. . . .
>
> Inside the complex, Nile River Road stretches between two rows of statutes of Egyptian royalty. Dominating the site are two pyramids that stand about 30 feet tall, visible from the two-lane road that winds past. A gold pyramid serves as a mini-mall, complete with a bookstore and apparel store. A four-column brown pylon marks the beginning of a winding labyrinth that leads to the entryway of the black pyramid, which serves as a church. Inside, an Egyptian-like chant hums over speakers 24 hours a day. The floors are covered with sand. The group's lodge, an elaborately painted white building trimmed in gold, doubles as a museum that houses artifacts ranging from busts of King Tut and Queen Nefertiti to a glass tomb holding an alien-like creature with a huge head and bulging eyes. A white obelisk, gold lamp posts, and stone animals make up a small African-like garden outside. . . .
>
> About 100 Nuwaubians live in single-wide mobile homes neatly aligned in a row behind the Egyptian-like architecture. (*Atlanta Journal-Constitution*, August 16, 1998)

The Yammassee Indian Tribe, also known as the United Nuwaubian Nation of Moors is under the leadership of Malachi Z. York. York has described himself as an angelic being. He is one of the Eloheem from the planet Rizq in the nineteenth galaxy of ILLYUWN who has come to earth in order save the chosen 144,000 Children of the Eloheem Annunaqi; the chosen are called Nuwaubians. According to York, the Eloheem have been visiting the earth for millennia. His current tenure on the planet began in 1970 when he incarnated the body of an earth man. He traveled the last leg of the journey to earth on a small passenger craft called a SHAM. The main leg of the journey was aboard the mother plane NIBIRU.

The NIBIRU has other purposes in visiting our planet, however. It has undertaken the task of moving the Crystal City of New Jerusalem from Orion to our own solar system. When that transport mission is complete, the NIBIRU will transport the 144,000 chosen to that space city, a process which itself will take forty years. In the Crystal City for 1,000 years, the chosen will then return to earth to battle the Luciferians and redeem humanity from the devil's control.

The Eloheem are not the only extraterrestrial beings to visit the earth, however. Some of them come to assist us in our development, some come to trade with us (thanks for the polio vaccine and the hula hoop!), some come as enemies of the human race. Among the ETs who visit earth regularly are the grays and the reptoid races. Some extraterrestrials come to earth to capture humans in order to satisfy their hunger. The aliens tend to prefer the purer, more tender meat of children. As York noted, 'This should make you stop and think, where are all those 'missing' children that appear on milk cartons? (Malachi Z. York, 'Is God an Extraterrestrial?', at http://www.factology.com/front4_15_00.htm). He also claims that the 'nectar of the gods' that is craved by extraterrestrials can only be found in freshly killed humans; it is the accumulation of adrenaline at the brain stem produced by terror. This 'nectar' is best when taken from children.

The Nuwaubians also believe that the earth is hollow and inhabited by various races of extraterrestrials. Some of these are quite familiar, the Teros and the Deros. One website of the Nuwaubian Nation offers this rather delightfully detailed description of the latter:

THE DEROS

This group of insane cave dwellers, were called sumuwnean, meaning 'the Obese Ones' or saamiym and ABANDONDEROS or as they are called today 'DEROS' which is a combination of the word 'DETRIMENTAL' and 'ROBOTS'. These Sumuwneans or deros really exist. Their chief is yabahaan. The sumuwneans are constantly in conflict with the group of beings called Duwanis who hold the same belief, that they too will take over the planet one day. They are born by hatching from eggs that are four to six feet in diameter. They grow to seven feet tall and are extremely Obese.

The Dero who live in the caves are degenerated so much that they don't have much intelligence. They have two stomachs and their digestive system is the same as that of a cow. Deros and Cows both chew the cud, meaning when cows eat, they chew their food and it goes through the initial stages of digestion where it reaches the a large sac that is before the true stomach. The food is then regurgitated to the mouth for further chewing; this is called chewing the Cud. The Deros have no Fingernails, Toenails, Nipples, Navels or Rectums. There [sic] eyes are Silver grey and they glow in the dark. They have blond eyebrows and Pinkish Grey Color Skin mutch [sic] like the corpse of a Caucasion, [sic] and a pig having not being exposed to the inner or outer sun. Other than their eyebrows, they have no hair on their bodies because of a disease called Trichotillomania, and are responsible for the disease Trichinosis and Trichiniasis. They have no teeth. Their mouth appears to be full of a gummy, slimy substance. They are Nocturnal and hear extremely well. They are not very peaceful and have a long dislike for human beings. They are very human in appearance, yet far from it. Their noses are long, trunk like which is very similar to that of an Elephant.

They contend that the planet Earth was Theirs Originally and will be theirs again one day. Many people today who are Obese Are Decendants [sic] of the deros. I'm talking about those people 300 Pounds and more, it is not normal for human beings. It is obviously a Heriditary Grandular [sic] problem and is caused by over active Glands, Certain Endocrine Gland Disorders, such as Hypothyroidism or tumors of the adrenal gland, Pancreas, or pituitary gland, can cause Obesity. It is a trait of the DEROS. THEY ARE FROM THE DEROS. (http://users.netropolis.net/ moorish/page12.htm)

York's theology is complicated by his insistence that the Nuwaubians who comprise the chosen 144,000 are descendants of ancient Egyptians who migrated to central Georgia long before the ancestors of the American Indians crossed the Bering Strait, making them the true Native Americans. Thus the Nuwaubians use both Egyptian and Native American symbolism to express their identity. Of course, they also claim to be extraterrestrial in origin. Taking elements from Islam, Christianity, and Judaism as well as from Richard Shaver and black nationalism, York has managed to create what is perhaps the most unique and syncretistic doctrine in all of ufology.

Unfortunately, the group has fallen on hard times following the conviction of York for child molestation. His attempts to avoid conviction because he is a member of the independent nation of the Yamassees have so far not been effective. The Egypt of the West has been deserted, though the Nuwaubians have in some ways been invigorated by their belief that York's conviction is an attempt by the forces of evil to destroy his work. They have rallied around him, attended his trials dressed in Native American garb, and turned his arrest into something of a cause for which to fight.

◆ ◆ ◆

In recent years the ancient astronauts have inserted themselves into the news cycle, but not in the way that Leslie, von Däniken or Sitchin would have led us to expect. Archeology has not uncovered the conclusive evidence that our ancestors were from the stars; the planet NIBIRU has not been spotted by astronomers on its way back toward earth; our god-like extraterrestrial ancestors have not appeared in spacecraft floating above the White House or Buckingham Palace. The ancient astronauts have been in the news in the form of their devotees, their believers, their champions. This has not served to move these groups into the mainstream, however. If anything, it has served to further marginalize them.

Tom Cruise launches a tirade against modern psychiatry on national television and reveals something about himself that he might not have wanted to show. Xenu and body thetans and auditing – these are things that the mainstream cannot grasp, they are alien concepts, making those who believe in these things alien as well. The Raelians announce that they have cloned a human being; investigation reveals the truth and the Raelians stand exposed –

UFO religion

Elohim and flying saucers: alien ideas held by alien minds. Michael York is arrested for child abuse and we hear of ET races that drink the adrenaline from the spinal cords of children. Alien thoughts held by aliens among us.

What is it to remain alienated in the media age, no longer consigned to pulp magazines and tabloid newspapers, but alienated even while on the evening news? What is it to be known and still unknown, understood and yet foreign? The faces seen on television screens, and movie screens, are alien faces. Not the Hollywood kind made of latex and make-up but the real kind, made of flesh and blood.

The religious movements talked about in this chapter, the Scientologists and the Raelians and the Nuwaubians, challenge our ability to accept things that are different, things that are alien, and not only because their ideas strike us as strange but perhaps also because they themselves scare us – Tom Cruise taking on psychiatry; Rael's free love; York's insistence that he is above and beyond the laws of the land; clumps and clusters of body thetans affixed to our souls; human clones with our transferred memories; aliens preying on our fear.

When we go to sleep at night we know that it is irrational to fear that aliens will enter our room while we sleep and perform acts about which we cannot speak. When we go to sleep at night we know that it is not irrational to fear that the other kind of aliens, the aliens among us, might threaten our hopes and our dreams. Heaven's Gate opens upon a world of fears – some justified, some not – about a future in which people hold that their beliefs and ethics are pure and true, straight from the stars. Such blind faith can lead to disaster, even war. Of course, it is not only gods from outer space who claim a monopoly on the truth, plenty of gods do that as well.

Conclusion
The New Gods?

Thus ends this Fortean parade of oddities, freaks, and monstrosities.

Tin-foil robots; tall, thin creatures warbling the marching tune; naked hippies from Mars; tiny humans with perfect teeth, their skin charred a chocolate brown; ghostly men dressed in black; mutilated cattle, drained of their blood; tall white denizens of the desert after dark; big-eyed grays with heads like chicken embryos, performing sinister operations; hybrid children, alien and human, their wispy blond hair blowing in the wind; tiny women the size of children, wearing boots and berets and marching like soldiers; long-haired, stunningly beautiful men; women without bras; women in electrified evening gowns; one-armed prophets; a crew of castrati; angels, Atlanteans, Elohim, and Anunnaki; reptilians and shapeshifters; Al Gore and George W. Bush; coagulated clumps of disembodied souls; human clones; black-skinned Indians; and, bringing up the rear, the Deros who chew the cud like cows, without fingernails, nipples, or rectums, noses like elephant trunks, skin the color of a Caucasian corpse, hairless, toothless, with mouths full of slime.

It is often said that the flying saucer phenomenon is an example of cold war hysteria. Fear of nuclear annihilation and of Russian rockets are offered as explanations for why people saw lights in the night sky. It was only Sputnik making personal appearances in suburban nightmares and rural dreamscapes. This is certainly how Hollywood interpreted the phenomenon. *Invasion of the Body Snatchers* and *Earth Versus the Flying Saucers* turned the fear of flying saucers and their occupants into a thinly veiled metaphor for McCarthy's red scare and post-Nagasaki nuclear neurosis. I suppose that some of this may be true. Perhaps the culture placed its fear of nuclear annihilation on those mysterious night time lights because the real terror was too much to face. Saucers may have been a substitute for nuclear warheads and Soviet satellites. There was certainly more going on than this, however; flying saucers were bigger than cold war paranoia. That explanation ignores too many of the facts, it ignores the longevity of the phenomenon and, most importantly, it ignores the diversity of responses to the flying saucers in our skies, a diversity that was present from the very beginning.

For those not willing to dismiss the phenomena as mass hallucinations and to simply discount the eyewitness accounts, I suppose that the most logical approach would have been to attempt an analysis of the phenomena, to treat UFO reports seriously and to evaluate them with the tools available from the physical sciences. In different ways, and with different levels of success, this is what the proponents of 'nuts and bolts' ufology attempted to do. Investigators such as Keyhoe, Edwards, and Hynek organized the testimony into a coherent system that could then be analyzed scientifically. For them the idea that the sightings were of physical craft piloted by extraterrestrials was a scientific hypothesis. Evidence should be gathered, cataloged, analyzed, and carefully presented. Eyewitness testimonies should be tested for reliability. Perhaps one day, Hynek suggested, scientists will understand the UFO phenomenon in the way that they now understand the aurora borealis, once a mystery of the heavens. Their approach was not driven by cold war hysteria, but by scientific materialism. It tried to explain visions and spectacles with empirical facts. Though the scientific technique employed was often amateurish, it was seldom anything but sincere.

The sightings could not be contained as scientific data, however, and no matter how much the nuts and bolts researchers would have liked to keep things empirical, that simply was not to be the case. Indeed, their own theories betrayed elements of a fear that showed itself in ufology more clearly with the passing of time. The nuts and bolts ufologists were afraid, but not necessarily of communism. They feared their own government and its secrets. Both Keyhoe and Edwards were convinced that the US government was keeping important secrets from the American public, that the government knew the truth about the saucers, about their extraterrestrial origin, and about their reasons for appearing in our skies.

Soon nuts and bolts ufology would be peopled by Men in Black, possibly alien beings and possibly government agents, who served more than anything to illustrate a connection between the two. The home base for this secret collaboration between the government and the aliens was none other than Area 51 which, whether it contained saucers or not, certainly contained a lot of scary secrets. Perhaps it is there that the secrets of Roswell are kept under lock and key. Even Hollywood's interpretation of the UFO phenomenon would come to reflect this. The movie *Independence Day* says the secrets of our government are so dark that even the president knows nothing about them. *The X-Files* makes the conspiracy – the connection between the aliens and the government – so complex that the secrets appear to be unknowable. In contrast to the classic interpretation of the saucer phenomenon, we are afraid, not of the Russians, but of ourselves. Men in Black, Tall Whites, Grays – the occupants of the saucers are in collusion with our government, mutilating cows and God only knows what else. Perhaps the government is even involved in the abduction of humans for experimentation and sexual abuse.

Of course, the fear of alien abduction is centered upon more than government abuses. This fear is more personal, more nightmarish, than the fear of conspiratorial bureaucracies. This fear comes to us in the night, while we are sleeping and most defenseless. Our bodies become paralyzed and our memories are erased; the things done to us are too hard for memory to hold. These stories must certainly play on a primal terror. It is the fear of the attack in the night, when defenses are down and the predators are prowling. It is also the fear of our own secret life, the parts of our souls that we don't even want to admit to ourselves, things only seen in our dreams and in our half-awake midnight epiphanies. This strikes me as scarier than the cold war. These fears are not focused on the other side of the Iron Curtain and don't go away with the fall of the Berlin Wall. These are fears that we have to live with, fears that keep us awake and that inhabit our dreams. Ironically, fear of the alien is fear of the self.

Not all responses to flying saucers have been so dark. The contactees also challenge the interpretation of the saucer flap as an expression of cold war anxiety, but not by offering up something else to fear. The contactees were not afraid of the alien forces filling the skies. Instead they were excited by the possibilities that the flying saucers and their occupants offered them. When George Adamski saw lights in the night sky he did not quake in fear of communist bombs. Rather, Adamski, Bethurum, Angelucci, and the others saw hope in the flying saucers and cigars. Interplanetary travel meant that the human species could improve, that things we dream of today are possible tomorrow. Most important of all, with technological development came moral development. The interstellar travelers bring a message of peace and of hope for tomorrow.

Not completely naive, the contactees claimed that the messages from alien beings contained warnings along with the promises. The contactees understood the danger of the bomb, the danger of war among technological societies, and the danger of racial division and hatred. Orfeo Angelucci was told to weep for his people, as Jesus wept for Jerusalem. Fear is not the same as hopelessness, however, and the aliens offered promises of what was possible if peace is pursued on the earth, if love replaces hatred, if faith replaces fear.

In a sense Orthon, Aura, and Borealis were new gods. Like the old gods they came from above, from the starry heavens. Like the old gods they bring warnings and promises. Unlike the old gods, however, they are human. Orthon is one of us, better than us for sure, but one of us. He is mortal. These new gods bring with them a hope that humanity can save itself, that we are not on the road to perdition, and that the discoveries of the atomic age do not have to end with the destruction of the earth but may take us into the future, take us to the stars. In contrast to the fear of government conspiracies and alien abductions, which reveal to us the fear we have of ourselves, the new gods of the contactees give us reason to believe that we can be better, that we can be gods, that we can live among the stars.

Unfortunately, the new gods have not always maintained their youth and their promise. Some of them have grown old. The gods of Heaven's Gate demanded blind obedience and self-sacrifice. They demanded that humans give up their humanity as if it were something to fear. Followers of these gods had to give up their lives in order to enter the gates of heaven. Their self-hatred led to castration; their desire to escape from this world led to death. All of this, of course, is done under the order of the gods. These gods don't seem all that new. They seem like the same old gods all over again, preaching self-hatred and fear.

The same path has been followed by those who look to the ancient past for the answer to the mysteries of life. The central claim of the ancient astronaut theory is that the stories of the gods are really stories about extraterrestrials. Among other things, this serves to bring the gods into our world, to make them more like ourselves. The gods are not the immortals of lore, not omniscient and omnipotent beings, but rather better versions of us. Von Däniken transforms the gods into humans and finds the answer to the mysteries of ancient civilizations in the literal stars rather than in the metaphorical heavens. Though betraying a lack of confidence in the abilities of the ancients themselves who need outside help to achieve their wonders, von Däniken does not place the source of that help beyond the empirical world. These gods, the gods of old, are new gods as well, ancient humans from the stars, giving us the hope of reaching the stars ourselves.

These gods also grow old, however, and begin to make accusations and demands. Not humanoid but reptoid, they show us the devil within ourselves. The old fall from grace makes us into beings encrusted with nearly infinite pain, our bodies nothing but magnets for sorrow, broken souls and body thetans. Strict rules, blind obedience, singular prophets with sole access to the message, a callous certainty concerning the truth of our convictions – these new gods, grown old, take us there too, but for one great moment they didn't. For one great moment there was room for Orthon, Alan, Ashtar, Aura, and Borealis. The past looked like it had never looked before, filled with, of all things, hope for the future. The future too looked new, the atom bomb behind us, the moon ahead.

I don't know what people have been seeing in the sky. I don't have any answer to the secret of the UFOs. I don't know if they are occupied by Venusians, Pleiadians, Soviets, or by nothing more than our own fantasies. I do know, however, that visions in the sky can tell us a great deal about ourselves, about both our hopes and our fears. As a child the aurora borealis terrified me; it conjured up all of my worst fears. Today, thankfully, a glimpse of it would bring only wonder. Both of these responses can be called responses to the holy, or if that is too big a word, responses to the infinite, the universe, to life itself. The way UFO cults and cultures have responded to flying saucers shows their, and our, response to life. These responses have been varied and complex. For some the response has been fear – of government, of themselves, of the future, of the unknown. For others the response has been blind devotion and obedience – to esoteric texts and teachings and to charismatic leaders. Still others have responded with hope and faith – sometimes even faith in ourselves and hope for our future. Sometimes, for brief moments and in unexpected places, the gods have been made new.

◆ ◆ ◆

The spring of my first-grade year did not bring an end to our fascination with saucers and 'Martians,' as we liked to call all ETs in those innocent days. (Sorry Venusians, Pleiadians, Nephilihim, and visitors from Clarion – the planet that lies beyond our moon!) The continued wave of sightings across the nation in the winter and spring of that year only elevated our six-year-old interests. The pinnacle of our saucer craze came on, of all days, St. Patrick's Day. Our teacher had carefully decorated our classroom so that as we arrived that morning we would see strange, tiny, green footprints covering the floors, the desks, and the walls. Clearly her intention was to suggest that leprechauns had explored our classroom while we were away. Ancient Celtic tradition notwithstanding, my friends and I would have none of that obviously mythological explanation. Leprechauns were fictional creatures mostly known to us from cereal boxes and the associated Saturday morning television commercials. (Frosted Lucky Charms, they're magically delicious!) They were no more real than Tony the Tiger or Toucan Sam. The footprints, we insisted, were not made by leprechauns. They were made by Martians.

Apparently giving up on her prepared lesson plan, our teacher let our more contemporary theory carry the day. At recess I led a group of young explorers as we searched the playground for evidence of the saucer landing site. We located their point of egress as an open window leading to a janitor's closet. We found strange burn marks on the tennis court, sure signs that weapons had been discharged. And the search did not end with the close of that school day. We resumed our quest on the next day, and the day after that. We would find the secret of our visitors if it took all year, if it took a lifetime. Pot of gold be damned, we were looking for something more precious than gold. We were looking for a source of wonder and awe that was right for us, the children of the space age, the children who took moon landings as a matter of course, the children who were already, at age six, too old for leprechauns. We promised that we would not give up until we found it. Though we now know the footprints were no more made by aliens than by greedy forest sprites and that real aliens, if there be any, would probably not descend to earth in pie plates and wrap themselves in tin foil, some of us have never given up the search . . .

Bibliography

Adamski, George (1949) *Pioneers of Space: A Trip to the Moon, Mars, and Venus* (Los Angeles, Leonard-Freefield)

—— (1955) *Inside the Space Ships* (New York, Abelard-Schuman)

Angelucci, Orfeo (1955) *The Secret of the Saucers* (Amherst, WI, Amherst Press)

Barker, Gray (1997) *They Knew Too Much about Flying Saucers* (Lilburn, GA, IllumiNet Press), first published 1956

Battaglia, Debbora (2005) *E. T. Culture: Anthropology in Outerspaces* (Durham, NC, Duke University Press)

Bender, Albert K. (1968) *Flying Saucers and the Three Men* (New York, Paperback Library)

Bennett, Colin (2001) *Looking for Orthon* (New York, Paraview Press)

—— (2002) *Politics of the Imagination: The Life, Work, and Ideas of Charles Fort* (Manchester, Critical Vision Press)

Berliner, Don and Stanton T. Friedman, (1992) *Crash at Corona* (New York, Marlowe Company)

Berlitz, Charles and William L. Moore (1980) *The Roswell Incident* (New York, MJF Books)

Bernard, Raymond (1964) *The Hollow Earth* (New York, Fieldcrest)

Bethurum, Truman (1954) *Aboard a Flying Saucer* (Los Angeles, DeVorss and Co.)

—— (1995) *Messages from the People of the Planet Clarion* (Scottsdale, AZ, Inner Light Publications)

Bramley, William (1993) *The Gods of Eden* (New York, Avon Books)

Chariton, Wallace O. (1991) *The Great Texas Airship Mystery* (Plano, TX, Wordware Publishing)

Cohen, Daniel (1981) *The Great Airship Mystery: A UFO of the 1890s* (New York, Dodd, Mead and Co.)

Colavito, Jason (2005) *The Cult of Alien Gods: H.P. Lovecraft and Extraterrestrial Pop Culture* (Amherst, NY, Prometheus Books)

Constable, Trevor James (1959) *They Live in the Sky* (Los Angeles, New Age Publications)

UFO religion

Corso, Philip J. (1997) *The Day after Roswell* (New York, Pocket Books)

Däniken, Erich von(1968) *Chariots of the Gods? Unsolved Mysteries of the Past* (New York, G.P Putnam's and Sons)

—— (1970) *Gods From Outer Space* (New York, Bantam Books)

—— (1972) *The Gold of the Gods* (New York, G. P. Putnam's Sons)

—— 1973) *In Search of Ancient Gods* (New York, G. P. Putnam's Sons)

Darlington, David (1997) *Area 51: The Dreamland Chronicles* (New York, Henry Holt and Co.)

David, Jay (1967) *The Flying Saucer Reader* (New York, New American Library)

Denzler, Brenda (2001) *The Lure of the Edge: Scientific Passions, Religious Beliefs, and the Pursuit of UFOs* (Berkeley, CA, University of California Press)

Edwards, Frank (1966) *Flying Saucers: Serious Business* (New York, Lyle Stuart)

—— (1967) *Flying Saucers: Here and Now* (New York, Bantam Books)

Fitzgerald, Randall (1998) *Cosmic Test Tube* (Los Angeles, Moon Lake Media)

Fort, Charles (1974) *The Complete Books of Charles Fort* (Mineola, NY, Dover Publications)

Fowler, Raymond E. (1979) *The Andreasson Affair: The Documented Investigation of a Woman's Abduction Aboard a UFO* (Newberg, OR, Wildflower Press)

—— (1993) *The Allagash Abductions: Undeniable Evidence of Alien Intervention* (Columbus, NC, Wild Flower Press)

Friedman, Stanton T. (1996) *Top Secret/MAJIC* (New York, Marlow and Company)

Friedrich, Mattern (1975) *UFOs: Nazi Secret Weapon* (Toronto, Samisdat Press)

Fry, Daniel (1992) *The White Sands Incident* (Madison, WI, Horus House), first published 1954

Fuller, John G. (1965) *The Interrupted Journey: Two Lost Hours 'Aboard a Flying Saucer'* (New York, Dial Press)

Gardner, Martin (1995) *Urantia: The Great Cult Mystery* (Amherst, NY, Prometheus Books)

Hall, Charles James (2002) *Millennial Hospitality* (1st Books)

Hopkins, Budd (1987) *Intruders: The Incredible Visitations at Copley Woods* (New York, Ballantine Books)

—— and Carol Rainey (2003) *Sight Unseen* (New York, Pocket Star Books)

Hubbard, L. Ron (2002) *Dianetics: The Modern Science of Mental Health* (Los Angeles, Bridge Publications)

Hynek, J. Allen (1972) *The UFO Experience: A Scientific Inquiry* (New York, Ballantine)

Icke, David (1999) *The Biggest Secret* (Scottsdale, AZ, Bridge of Love Books)

Jacobs, David M. (1992) *Secret Life: Firsthand Documented Accounts of UFO Abductions* (New York, Simon and Schuster)

Keith, Jim (1997) *Casebook on the Men in Black* (Lilburn, GA, IllumiNet Press)

Keyhoe, Donald E. (1950) *The Flying Saucers Are Real* (New York, Fawcett Publications)

Korff, Kal K. (1995) *Spaceships of the Pleiades: The Billy Meier Story* (Amherst, NY, Prometheus Books)

Layne, Meade (1950) *The Ether Ship and its Solution* (California, Borderland Sciences)

Leslie, Desmond and George Adamski (1953) *Flying Saucers Have Landed* (New York, The British Book Centre)

Lewis, James R., ed. (1995) *The Gods Have Landed: New Religions From Other Worlds* (Albany, NY, State University of New York Press)

—— (2003) *The Encyclopedic Sourcebook of UFO Religions* (Amherst, NY, Prometheus Books)

Mack, John E. (1994) *Abduction: Human Encounters with Aliens* (New York, Ballantine Books)

Menger, Howard (1959) *From Outer Space to You* (New York, Pyramid Books)

Moffitt, John F. (2003) *Picturing Extraterrestrials: Alien Images in Modern Mass Culture* (Amherst, NY, Prometheus Books)

Moosbrugger, Guido (2004) *And Still They Fly!* (Tulsa, OK, Steelmark)

Moseley, James W. and Karl T. Pflock (2002) *Shockingly Close to the Truth: Confessions of a Grave-Robbing Ufologist* (Amherst, NY, Prometheus Books)

Norman, Ernest L. (1956) *The Infinite Concept of Cosmic Creation* (El Cajon, CA, Unarius Educational Foundation)

—— (1956) *The Voice of Venus* (El Cajon, CA, Unarius Educational Foundation)

Norman, Ruth (1987) *Preparation for the Landing* (El Cajon, CA, Unarius Educational Foundation)

Palmer, Susan J. (2004) *Aliens Adored: Rael's UFO Religion* (New Brunswick, NJ, Rutgers University Press)

Partridge, Christopher, ed. (2003) *UFO Religions* (London, Routledge)

Persuitte, David (2000) *Joseph Smith and the Origins of the Book of Mormon*, 2nd edition (Jefferson, NC, McFarland and Company)

Rael (2005) *Intelligent Design* (Nova Distribution)

UFO religion

Randle, Kevin D. and Donald R. Schmitt (1991) *UFO Crash at Roswell* (New York, Avon Books)

Saler, Benson, Charles A. Ziegler, and Charles B. Moore (1997) *UFO Crash at Roswell: The Genesis of a Modern Myth* (Washington, DC, Smithsonian Institution Press)

Scully, Frank (1950) *Behind the Flying Saucers* (New York, Henry Hold and Company)

Silverberg, Robert (1968) *The Mound Builders* (Athens, OH, Ohio University Press)

Sitchin, Zecharia (1990) *Genesis Revisited* (New York, Avon Books)

Smith, Toby (2000) *Little Gray Men: Roswell and the Rise of a Popular Culture* (Albuquerque, NM, University of New Mexico Press)

Streiber, Whitley (1987) *Communion: A True Story* (New York, Avon Books)

Urantia Foundation, The (1955) *The Urantia Book* (Chicago, Urantia Foundation)

Williamson, George Hunt (1990) *Other Tongues, Other Flesh* (Albuquerque, NM, BE Books)

Index